Foreword By Dan Kennedy

BUSINESS KAMASUTRA

From Persuasion to Pleasure

Parthiv Shah

Manufactured in the United States of America.

ISBN: 978-0-9905059-2-1

A PRAYER FOR EVERY ENTREPRENEUR

This is a true story. In February of 2002, when I left Perrone to start ListLaunchers, we had a prayer ceremony at our new office just before we actually moved into it. There, sitting on the floor in the presence of my family, friends, and some business associates, the priest said the following prayer. I still remember every word of it as if it were yesterday:

"You have now embarked on a new journey by starting this business. For the next one thousand days, we the family, we the religion, we the society, relieve you of all your earthly responsibilities. Now this is your place of work. This is your place of worship; this your home; this is your playground. Sit down; get to work, and for the next one thousand days, commit your heart and soul to focusing on making this work. At the end of one thousand days, you will be a successful businessman, a better family man, a better religious man, and a philanthropist who will be committed to make the world a better place!"

I want to start this book by saying this prayer for all my fellow entrepreneurs. May God bring you the same success he has brought to me and my family!

Sincerely,

Parthiv Shah, President
<u>eLaunchers.com</u>

FOREWORD

IF YOU LAID ALL THE BUSINESS BOOKS PUBLISHED THIS YEAR END TO END, you could probably walk to Mars and back—and be mind-numbed by the sameness and redundancy of so many of them. I write business books myself, so I am sensitive to the difficult challenge of breaking new ground. Of having a legitimate reason for existence, other than being a published author. It's not an easy hurdle to overcome the sameness. Most don't. Most can be ignored. Parthiv Shah's little book, *Business Kamasutra*, should not be.

"BUSINESS IS SEX" is a different, provocative idea. When he ran it by me, I encouraged Parthiv to, pardon the pun, flesh it out, and he has done so brilliantly and concisely. I have often said that marketing done well may be the most fun you can have with your clothes on. I co-authored one book on selling with a former, famous 'madam.'

Most of my strategies focus on attraction in place of pursuit, and consent in place of rape. I was practicing and preaching this long, long before phrases like "permission marketing" were popularized by others in corporate America. This little book puts structure and system and technology for implementation underneath these ideas.

THE CHIEF PROBLEM with which most business operators—small and large—wrestle is not understanding what needs to be done. Smart owners, professionals and executives get past that. But when they understand the dance they need to do with the prospective customer, client, patient or donor, the seduction they need to succeed at, they are ahead of competitors only in understanding. And having only better understanding is akin to knowing 365 different sexual positions but staying home alone every night. IMPLEMENTATION separates those who score from those who don't. It's never just what you know, it's what you do, get done, can get done by others and by automation, and can get done right consistently. Parthiv is an implementor. He has, bluntly, a clever thief inside him, that I am not always comfortable with, but then, the "swipe and deploy", the aggregation of best strategies is what is often incorrectly characterized as "innovation." Innovation is far too highly prized, when it is implementation that matters most. Schultz didn't invent the coffee shop, and freely admits taking "inspiration" from European bistros. Jobs did not invent the computer—he mastered the merchandising of it as no one else ever has. Kroc did not invent the hamburger stand or "fast food." This book gets from concepts to practical implementation. Which is where you want to be.

"Business Is Sex" is a really great conceptual way to understand relationships with prospects and customers, but without the methodology and means and resources of implementing, it's empty.

COMPLEXITY IS EMBRACED in this book, and enabled by the suggestions late in this book. A current pet peeve of mine is the childish pursuit of simplicity. Businesses build sustainable advantage with complexity, not with simplicity. McDonalds is currently suffering in part because it is too simple a business, thus easily chewed at by countless copycat competitors. Disney is thriving because it is an incredibly complex business ecosystem. PROCESS COMPLEXITY is an extremely valuable asset. As the Kama Sutra greatly complicates sex but gives its master dramatic advantage in sustaining the interest of his lover(s), the ability to implement this Business Kamasutra gives sustainable competitive advantage to a company.

Too many business books are nothing but flowery words and foreplay, a romancing, with no consummation. Here, Parthiv has provided method and means for consummating change in your business.

Dan S. Kennedy
Marketing Strategies and Consultant.
Author, No B.S. book series including *No B.S. Guide to Ruthless Management of People and Profits.*
www.NoBSBooks.com

PARTHIV SHAH

Parthiv Shah is president and founder of eLaunchers.com and a serial entrepreneur. He has been an implementation craftsman and data scientist all his life. He started his career in direct mail marketing in 1989. Shah learned tricks of the trade from direct mail guru Matt Perrone while working at J. M. Perrone Company in Hingham, MA from 1989 to 2002. Shah started a dot-com company in 1999, failed to make it a success, went back to work for the direct mail company, and left again to start ListLaunchers in 2002 with offices in Pembroke, MA. ListLaunchers started out as a mailing list company helping printers, mail houses, direct marketers, fundraisers, and ad agencies with their list research & data acquisition needs. It evolved into a full-service online/offline marketing campaign implementation firm specializing in automotive marketing. Shah sold ListLaunchers to an Indian Info Tech company and started eLaunchers.com in 2006. Meeting Bill Glazer in 2009 was a game changer for Shah.

This new company, eLaunchers.com, is a turnkey sales, lead generation, and marketing company that helps small and not-so-small-businesses and organizations compete against rivals, who have deep pockets and large marketing budgets. The eLaunchers.com team has developed a data-driven direct marketing process that integrates e-mail, direct mail, and web advertisements. eLaunchers.com has established itself as a Done-For-You Implementation company, helping small to mid-sized businesses experience a transformational marketing makeover given fifteen days of preparation time and typically 48 days of buildout. The entire game is played on WordPress, Infusionsoft, membership sites, SQL tables, PURL engine, and some custom object-oriented programming. Shah is passionate about helping small businesses grow.

eLaunchers.com has a global workforce—with marketing and data experts in America and API developers, mobile app developers, object-oriented programmers, and Web/CRM implementation specialists in other countries.

Shah has a passion for small business, with a soft corner in his heart for start-ups and not-yet-started start-ups. He helps small businesses develop their value proposition and identify market segments most suitable to their strengths.

Shah taught marketing and e-business to MBA students at the University of Phoenix MBA School of Business.

Originally from India, he migrated to the US in 1989 and lived with his family in Randolph, Massachusetts, a little south of Boston. He started a company, ListLaunchers.com that was bought out in 2005, and that acquisition brought him to Washington DC. He lives in Boyds, Maryland, about two miles away from his office. In 2014 eLaunchers.com purchased the office space in Germantown that became home to the eLaunchers.com Corporate Headquarters.

He has a passion for business, and he does a lot of pro bono marketing consulting work for fellow entrepreneurs. He enjoys community work and loves helping fellow entrepreneurs. He has also started five small businesses—including one internet start-up. In addition, because of the nature of his business, he works on hundreds of different business models every year and experiments with/contributes to their revenue model. For over eighteen years, he has worked in the direct marketing industry and lived through thousands of case studies. Throughout his career, he has mailed over a billion pieces of direct mail and brought in over fifteen million dollars in business to his companies.

He has a bachelor's degree in sociology from Gujarat State University and an MBA in marketing from Bentley College.

BOOK BONUS: To read the rest of Shah's books online and to request his Implementation Success Blueprint along with the companion CD, visit Shah's Virtual Library at http://www.dentalgrowthmachine.com/.

ANATOMY OF SEX

B TO B RELATIONSHIP AND B TO C RELATIONSHIP

1. Segmentation (Pick with whom you want to mate)

2. Approach (Plan, Orchestrate, Execute)

3. Acquire Consent (Establish trust)

4. Date before you mate (Measure trust, Manage trust)

5. Getting to know you... (Establish information sharing protocol, Understand what information drives the relationship)

6. Acquiring consent for intimacy (Importance of identifying the moment when it is appropriate to proceed 'further')

7. Falling in Love (Emotion will always outweigh attraction)

8. Foreplay (Preparing to engage, Treat them in a way that matters to them)

9. Mating (Intimacy without pleasure is meaningless, Focus on experience—not just the act)

10. Aftermath (How to take the experience of initial transaction into a lifelong mutually profitable relationship)

11. Stay in Love (How you make them feel will determine the longevity of the relationship)

ROLE OF DATA IN THE RELATIONSHIP (BUSINESS, WAR & SEX)

1. Why "Big Data" is the common element between the Business Relationship & Sex

2. Capture, catalogue, analyze, and display data that builds a relationship

3. Using data to manage turbulence in a relationship

4. Men are not from Mars. Women are not from Venus. It's just data that is not formatted properly

5. When you stop sharing data, relationships experience turbulence

ANATOMY OF TRUST:

LET DATA BE YOUR TRUST-O-METER

1. Establish Trust

2. Measure Trust

3. Manage Trust

4. Monitor Trust

5. Monetize Trust

6. Maintain Trust

7. Transfer of Trust: Testimonials & Referrals

MY MESSAGE

Businesses are born very much like human beings. People date, they mate, then they get pregnant with a business idea. They remain pregnant with the idea for a while, and one day, the business is born. The newborn baby instantly transforms you into the role of a parent. You have to feed the baby, nurture the baby, and take care of the baby. Sometimes when the baby cries in the middle of the night, you have to wake up and take care of whatever the baby needs.

Unfortunately, the infant mortality rate is very high in this segment. Most small businesses fail; however, most failures are avoidable. If we can help a small business survive the initial risk of failure, the baby can live a very long life. It will grow up and make a contribution to the life of the business owners. This now successful business becomes a home for the people hired by the company and makes a positive contribution to our economy and our nation. The most patriotic thing you can do is to start a business and succeed!

Most businesses just don't know how to date and mate. When seeking a soul mate, or even just a mating partner, humans work hard to segment the market, identify the right prospect, plan-prepare-orchestrate, and execute a perfect approach. They seek consent, engage in a dating ritual where both parties share information about each other, and establish trust. At some point, they reach a place in the relationship where they seek consent for intimacy, engage in foreplay, and then, when it feels right and when both players are ready, engage in the mating activity.

What would the life of a business look like if it followed this precious path to build relationships with its prospects, customers, marketing channels, and affiliates? What if the company can use data intelligence and big data for segmentation, multi-step direct marketing to plan-prepare-orchestrate and execute a "perfect" approach? What if it can use landing pages and online/offline bait to seek consent?

What if it can utilize marketing automation to engage in a dating ritual to send information to prospects and use surveys to gather information? Perhaps, it can employ technology-enabled trust-building tools to establish, measure, monitor, manage, maintain, and monetize trust. Things could reach a point in the relationship where the right to ask for an order is not just earned but has been long awaited.

With all this happening, the business can then engage in foreplay using a variety of tools and tactics. Things like shock and awe packages, a video marketing library, and chairside marketing material. This can also include the tasteful use of paper, pixel, and plastic to facilitate the lead capture and lead conversion.

Does your business go: brand development, interject some segmentation, then approach and attempt to mate? If this is your process, how will your business compete with a sophisticated competitor, who is using standardized and systematized marketing automation to facilitate the lead capture? Not only that, but how about leading nurture and relationship development before converting the leads into a lifelong relationship?

INTRODUCTION

There is a lot written on the subject of business and information. The reality is business and data can be a dull, boring, unsexy, and difficult-to-understand subject. Anyone who understands how human beings behave in a business-to-business relationship or a business-to-consumer relationship can position themselves in front of an opportunity in a meaningful way. If you show up in the right way, at the right place, at the right time, you will win the battle.

The name of this book is *Business Kamasutra*, but there is absolutely nothing here that is vulgar or inappropriate, or that cannot be read in the presence of your family.

This is the workflow I use to explain the anatomy of the relationship between two businesses. Businesses are born very much like human beings. People date; they mate, and they get pregnant with an idea of a business. Like an infant in the womb, they remain pregnant with an idea, until finally the business is born.

This newly born baby instantly puts you in a parenting mode. You have to help the business grow, you have to feed the baby, nurture it, assist it through puberty, and one day the baby will grow up and graduate. When that day dawns, it will make their parents proud.

Here is the problem with this analogy. The infant mortality rate is very high in this segment. Most small businesses fail.

The tragedy is that most failures are avoidable. If you can help a small business survive during its infancy, it will live for a very long time. It will do really well for its creator, the community it touches, the people it hires, and the customers it serves.

It is a very patriotic thing to start a business and actually become successful. So, let's talk about what matters. What matters are relationships. People buy from people they like. They choose to purchase or become involved with people they trust.

People buy emotionally, and they justify rationally. You, as a business owner, have an obligation to understand your constituents and build a relationship.

This book uses sex, a relationship between two humans, as a metaphor to describe a standardized and systematized workflow that defines rules of engagement to establish a genuine connection between businesses and their customers.

TABLE OF CONTENTS

SEX & BUSINESS

Business is not war; business is sex. In the history of business books and business relationships, a lot of books are written on the subject of warfare and the battle for market share. A lot of parallels are drawn between World War I and World War II and the battle for market share between Pepsi and Coke.

If you look at Harvard Business School's case studies, you will find numerous articles written on the subject of marketing myopia, marketing warfare, the battle for market share, and so on, and so forth.

There is a lot written on the subject of the theory of competitive relativity. If you are running from a tiger, you don't have to outrun the tiger; you just have to outrun the other guys in front of you. Every businessman is taught to take what they want and violently protect what they have because someone wants what they possess.

This hostile way of life is no way to live. This is not how business should be conducted. Business is not about taking. Business is not about deceptively convincing someone to give you what you want. Business is much more than that.

A business failure hurts. Business failure is scary. Ask me how I know. I have been dead-broke three times and in bankruptcy once, but none of those situations was due to a lack of business. All those were for having made bad business decisions.

So let us shift our focus to the conquest of owning a space.

In this book, you will find the concept of understanding relationships between businesses and their prospective clients or customers is very much like understanding how relationships are built between two humans.

As the title of this book indicates, business is a lot like sex. Let's talk about sex. How does it work? Well, the first step is segmentation. You don't want to sleep with just anybody, you want to be picky about who you choose as a potential mate. This goes beyond who your buyer is and what they buy, we will get to that in Chapter 1.

Once you know who you are and once you know who you want to go after, you can organize, orchestrate, and execute an approach. That's going to be discussed further in following Chapters.

Once you approach someone, what happens? Will they ignore you? Will they like you and give you consent to continue a conversation? Or, will they get upset that you had the audacity to approach them? Do they ignore you as though you don't exist? Or, after realizing your approach was not to their liking they turned their back on you? All of these possible scenarios are indeed that; possible.

If something negative occurs, so be it. That's okay. If you are not meant to be together, be considerate and cordially accept the "No, thank you" and move on. The world is filled with other opportunities, and we will talk about the approach and how to know when to give up. Have patience, we'll get to that.

Let's now assume you are successful in persuading someone to raise their hand and say "yes." They are interested in talking to you. Now what do you do? They didn't give you consent to mate; they gave you consent for a first date. That in itself is a small victory. So, smile and date. If you treat your new friend well, you just might get a second and third date.

In the other chapters, we are going to talk about monetization of trust. That's the mating part. Hopefully dating and courtship will reach a point where you get consent for intimacy. You are approaching a point where you are about to get consent to get intimate. When you finally get this consent, you are ready to mate. It is a very delicate moment, what do you do?

You want to make sure that the process is filled with pleasure. Let's talk about when you experienced pleasure during your last interaction with a business. Think. Was an experience at Starbucks pleasant? Was an experience at the Marriott pleasant? Was an experience at the local Walmart pleasant? Was an experience at the BMW dealership service department pleasant? Was an experience of buying a used car pleasant? Was an experience of working with your dentist pleasant? Was an experience of purchasing a plane ticket pleasant? Was an experience of getting on that plane and getting off the plane pleasant?

In the chapter called Foreplay, we will talk about what it takes to make someone happy and prepare them for mating and make the experience pleasurable. What happens if the experience is not pleasurable? Well, if you are the only game in town, they will stay.

However, if they are doing business with you but you constantly agitate and annoy them, things simply won't work out. They will be proactively looking for a supplier who can take care of them. Even if they are not annoyed, they are still being approached by other prospects. You will lose your customers to a better-looking supplier who promises a better experience.

People buy emotionally, and they justify rationally. It's normal human behavior. They are your client because it makes sense to them at the present moment, but they will talk to someone else because it gives them pleasure to do so. Most humans believe that the grass is always greener on the other side of the fence. But, if your process is filled with pleasure and they are enjoying the caresses you share, they will give you a tight hug back. They will repel your competition. They will keep buying from you. They will buy more. They will generate a better relationship. We'll talk about what foreplay and mating are comprised of in the next chapter.

In the following chapter, we are going to talk about the aftermath of mating. You need to provide good value in exchange for the money you are taking. Otherwise, the Business Kamasutra process will not work. The foundation of the Business Kamasutra framework is to spend enough time, energy, resources, and money to make someone comfortable, establish a relationship, and capitalize on that relationship.

If your deliverables are shallow and if you are unable to please your constituents in a meaningful way, you will not be able to monetize your relationships. You cannot afford to do segmentation; organize, orchestrate and execute your approach; get consent, build relationship; and do the whole dating routine. You cannot make them comfortable when they are ready to mate; you have to engage in foreplay before mating; then, mate. Too much time, money, and effort are at stake if you cannot build a long-term relationship with your customer.

And at last we will talk about having babies. In the framework of Business Kamasutra, the term "having babies" means asking your customers to help you build your world. You have babies by asking for referrals and asking them to usher you into relationships where you can do business with someone they already know, like, and trust.

If they can invite you into relationships, you will not have to work so hard to organize, orchestrate, and execute an approach.

The dating ritual will be shorter; foreplay will be more pleasurable for you and your clients, and mating will be more meaningful. Building relationships and seeking referrals from existing customers is the end game, the desired goal state of the Business Kamasutra framework.

SEGMENTATION

Segmentation in the Business Kamasutra framework is not the typical list research, market segmentation, and all that stuff. This goes way beyond that.

So, before we get into the nitty-gritty of it, let us focus on who you are. You don't want to sleep with just anybody. Again, going back to mating, the first thing is you want to be picky about who you want to select. Otherwise, you will end up with someone that you don't want to be with. First, let's figure out who you are, what you are, and why you are.

Simon Sinek wrote a book called *Start with Why*. I urge you to read it. Get a copy and dive right in. It is an amazing framework for soul-searching for a business. In the book, he talks about how Apple differentiated itself. If you know who you are, if you will know who you are for, and if you know how you want to be seen then you can advertise that and give yourself direction towards your target clientele. Think of this as being like your dating profile on an online dating site. So, define who you are, define what you are, and define why you are. This is not your unique selling proposition. This is much more divine, much more spiritual, much deeper than your USP. Put away everything you learned from Sandler Sales Institute and your entire sales training. For a moment, be independently wealthy; you don't need the next deal that comes to you. If you can choose to do business with who you want to do business with, who would that be? And how do you want that person to perceive you? What is your own perception of you and your business and your company? What are you? What is your DNA? What is your value proposition? What are your core values? What matters to you? What is your definition of victory? What is your definition of a home run? What can you do for your customers, clients, or patients that makes for a meaningful impact?

Once you understand who you are, what you are, why you are, what you do, and what it does it for your ideal customer, you are now ready to ask the next set of evaluations. Who you are for? Who is the ideal consumer for whatever it is you do?

For example, if you are a dentist who is your ideal patient? Is it an elderly couple who wants to get a pair of dentures?

Or is it a 27-year-old mom who needs to come in with her twins to see if they need braces?

As Simon Sinek says, *"If you start with your why and if your why is really well-defined, you will be able to naturally, flawlessly, and smoothly transition into defining who you are for."*

Once you determine who you are for, you'll need to determine how you want to be perceived? What do you want them to say about you to their friends and family? How do you want them to see you? How do you want them to value you? What is their definition of them liking you? This might require not just soul-searching but some serious market research, surveys, or asking heart-to-heart questions to your existing customers and even lost customers. These are people who you used to do business with, those that stopped their relationship with you. Ask them what would make them fall in love with you again? What do they want to see?

Once you have that data, ask yourself another question. Do you have the capacity to please your constituents in the way they want to be pleased?

Back to the formula. Who you are? What you are? Why you are? What do you do? What does it do for your ideal constituents? Who is your ideal constituent? How do they find you valuable? What is their definition of victory in your relationship? Do you have the capacity to please that constituent in that light? And are you willing to live with what that constituent is willing to give you in exchange for the value that you provide?

Remember, you cannot take a dime more than what you deserve. The universe has a way of figuring out when the value traded doesn't match the price paid. You might get lucky; you might be able to get away with it for a day or a week or a month or a year—maybe even a decade—, but eventually it will catch up to you. The universe must maintain balance.

Therefore, for the sake of sustainability and a universe that is built on that strong solid foundation, make sure that the relationship that you wish to build with the world is not going to be off kilter.

You don't want to go through a separation with your client that you fell in love with, do you? Think how hard it will be. Think how bad it will hurt. Think back; do you have relationships that you lost that you are still mourning? Yes, these are the relationships that I am talking about. How did you lose those relationships? Is it that you were not meant to be together? Were you chasing something that you did not deserve to chase? Did you land something that you did not deserve to land? You will get lucky, but you have an obligation to accept cautiously only what belongs to you and only do what you deserve to do.

A relationship that cannot last a lifetime isn't a relationship worth building. In business, you don't "mate" for the simple act for mere pleasure, you must "mate" to build a lifelong relationship. Because if all you need is a one-night stand, you don't need Business Kamasutra.

If that's the kind of person you are, I would like you to return this book to me, and I will FedEx a refund check. I will buy the book back from you because this is not for you. This framework will not work for you.

APPROACH

Now that you know what you are, why you are, who you are for, and how you want to please them and now that you have the capacity to please them, you can happily accept what you get in return when you please them. You know now that you want to build a lifelong relationship with these people. This relationship's value is more than any one-night-stand could ever be. You are ready to take the next step.

You want to organize, orchestrate, execute, and approach. We'll talk about these four words for a moment or two. Organize means that you want to think about strategizing what your approach is going to be. There are three thoughts to organizing the approach. Dan Kennedy talks about this in great detail in his book *NO B.S. Direct Marketing*.

I call it the first book of direct marketing. The three parts of organizing an approach are market, message, and media. In the earlier chapter, we talked in detail about who your market is going to be. That is the foundation of the Business Kamasutra framework.

Now that you know who your market is, let's focus on your message. Stephen Covey once said, in *Seven Habits of Highly Effective People*, to begin with the end in mind. So, let us begin with the end in mind. When you approach someone for the first time, what are you looking for?

What is your definition of victory? You want them to give you consent to date, hold hands maybe, and maybe even give you a first kiss. You don't want to be too aggressive when you approach someone for the first time, and your message should reflect that. Herein lies the difference between being a soft, subtle relationship builder and a fraud or self-centered individual. People don't like salespeople who only want to sell you stuff. It is nice to buy, but people don't like to be sold. So don't sell; just be available, but be in front of people in a meaningful way. Your message should reflect it. If you are an orthodontist, your message should not be $500 discount off on an Invisalign treatment. Rather, it should say, "Does your child need braces?"

If you are a dentist, your message should not be about a free exam, free x-ray, and $39 cleaning. Your message should be a consumer guide to dentistry. If you are a major case implant dentist, your message should not be about a $1000 discount on all implants. Your message should be about the true cost of losing a tooth.

Oh! What a difference a tooth makes in your life. Just ask someone who does not have all their teeth. If you are a pediatric dentist, you don't want to talk about buy-one-get-one-free, you want to take about teaching your kid how to brush and floss correctly to instill a habit.

Your message should be celebratory. Your message should be gifting. Your message should be giving something of substance and value in exchange for their contact information and consent to have a conversation.

Remember, when you approach someone for the first time, you have only a few seconds to say something engaging and get their attention.

People consume information differently. Some people only read, some people will watch videos. Some people will listen to streaming audio and CDs, and some people will go online and watch series of videos. We all have our unique ways of absorbing information, and we all have our own quirks. We'll talk about that in the following chapters. When you are building your message, your message should be able to be cohesively delivered in any media.

Okay, let us go back to the relationship between two humans. When you approach someone for the very first time, what do you say? Do you show off your stuff? Or do you compliment them on what they have? What do you say beyond hello?

You want to know about their situation. You should seek what they want to know about you; then, you tell them exactly what they want to hear. How do you do that? Do you go in with just one message, or do you have a whole bunch of messages ready to go? You deploy the message that they want to see, hear, read or consume based on the information that they gave you. That information will resonate because they have an interest in exactly what they offered up front. You supply it, and you're home free.

Now, let us think about who you are, what you are, and why you are from the previous chapter. My guess, you are probably more affluent than your client. You are certainly far more knowledgeable than your prospect or client is about the subject matter in which you are an expert.

What do you have that you are willing to give away? Do you possess valuable information geared specifically to help your ideal prospect or customer? Is there evidence that you are an expert? Do you possess data or something of substance and value that can improve their lives in some fashion? Is there evidence that you are an expert? Can you give them something of substance and value that can make a meaningful difference in their life? Is there a gift or something that you can give?

Remember, you want to give before you take. That is a way to build a relationship. When you reach out, your message should reflect that you want to give them something. For example, "the special reason for my calling today is I want to give you—fill in the blank" or "Pardon my intrusion by this email, but I thought you might want to read about what I came across that is relevant to your situation."

When you voluntarily reach out to someone, unsolicited, with a welcome gift, you are not an annoying and unwanted pest. Nobody wants solicitation; nobody wants someone knocking on their door saying, "Hey look at my stuff." Your message needs to reflect that you are sharing a gift that you believe they will find valuable. Your message also needs to have a clear call to action for the next step. This is called bait.

We will talk about call to action, bait, and the offer in the next segment, when we talk about orchestrating your approach.

Now that we talked about message, let us talk about the media. Remember, the triangle is market, message, and media.

People consume information differently. Some people will only read, and some people will only listen. There are some people that absorb information by way of visual learning Some people want to be told, and you just don't know how they are going to react.

Tony Robbins wrote a whole lot of stuff on the subject of NLP, or neurolinguistic programming. If you can understand and identify someone's information traits and if you communicate with them in the same way, it will be easier for you to build a rapport. The concept is also referred to as matching and mirroring. You want to talk to the person in a way that they talk because that is their definition of normal. If they speak slowly and methodically, match that pace, or you'll not connect.

In a general sense, there are three kinds of people: visual people, auditory people, and kinesthetic people. For example, if someone is watching your video and says, "I hear you," or if you send someone an email and they respond to you saying, "I hear you," talk to them– they are auditory people. If you are talking to someone explaining the concept and they say, "I see what you mean," stop talking and start showing stuff– they are visual people. Kinesthetic people want to interact with you. They want to touch your toys; they want to play with your knickknacks. They want to get a demo of your website or get a feel for what you are saying, so a simple message will not work.

These are the people who respond better to a shock and awe package that has a stuffed toy or a blanket or a coffee mug loaded with sugar-free chocolates. So, your shock and awe package needs to cater to all kinds of people. When you build your marketing mix or when you build your media package, you want to be mindful of how different people will consume your information and be prepared for all of it.

You want to have your message in audio. You want to have your message in video. You want to have your message in print. You want to have your message in an interactive format that consumers can play with, and you want to have some touchy-feely stuff that accompanies your message, so you can approach your target consumers with one cohesive force.

The best way to build a multimedia message is to start with video. Mike Stewart has a program called tablet video training. It teaches you how to build a 5-minute or 6-minute video using your iPad. Just speak your message in front of a video, using iMovie on iPad; then, quickly edit your message. Now, you have your message on a video.

Have the video message transcribed. There are companies that will transcribe your message for a very affordable fee. You can find them online quite easily; try Upwork or Fiverr.

You now have a video and a printed document. Take the video and transform that into an audio file (an mp3 file), and now you have an audio message. Now that you have the raw material of your message, you can give the transcript of your message to a curator, editor, and graphic designer, who can display the message to reflect a high-quality piece. The audio file can go on a website, or it can be recorded on a CD, so you can give someone a bonus CD with your letter. The video message can go on a video book, on a website, or on a DVD that you send out.

Now that you have your message in multiple mediums, let's talk about media. Media is just the delivery mechanism to get your message into the hands of the right people. How are you going to reach people?

We already know that people will respond differently to media they resonate with in your marketing mix. You want a multimedia marketing campaign.

How do you control the budget? Well, you control the budget by controlling your market segmentation. You cannot please everyone; therefore, do everything for a small number of people.

See, instead of just doing Facebook advertising and reaching out to the masses, identify a narrow segment of the market that you want to target, and put together a multimedia, multi-touch, micro-marketing campaign. You want to attack so fiercely that they can love you, they can hate you, but they cannot ignore you. You want to go at it with everything you've got.

What are your options in terms of selecting the proper medium to distribute your message? You can certainly do radio, television, print advertising, and public relations. You can also use direct mail marketing.

Now, direct mail can be very, very powerful—if you do your list work right. If you have a good handle on lists, you can do a multi-step direct mail campaign. The post office is very sophisticated, and you can send almost anything.

You can send a VHS video cassette tape that has your message on it and say, "If you no longer have a video cassette recorder, go online to watch the same video." That would be creative. Nobody has VHS tapes anymore. You can send a DVD. You can send a video book. You can send a pop-up letter. You can send a handwritten letter. You can send a three-dimensional (3D) mail piece. You know, a lumpy package or envelope. You can also send your messaging in a high-image envelope. If you want the resources, go to www.3dmailresults.com, and you can see around 185 examples of how inexpensive three-dimensional knickknacks can be. Send 3D mail accompanied by a well-written sales letter. It can produce meaningful results because of the novelty of the lumpy envelope or unusual container. People are curious by nature, so you are indirectly touching an emotional trigger just by getting them to open the envelope or package.

We've talked about organizing your approach. Now, let us talk about orchestrating your approach. What are you looking to accomplish when your message is delivered?

You obviously want them to respond to your message. You want them to take the next step. You want them to raise their hand and say they are interested. You want them to say, "Let's talk."

Keep in mind, while people receive information differently, people respond differently too. You want to have multiple channels of response mechanisms.

You want to have a business reply mail piece, so they can send back their reply sheet or reply card. You want to have a fax number, so they can fax back a response. (Yes, some people still use them.)

You want to have a landing page, so they can go online, respond to your offer, and get instant gratification. You might want to use personalized URLs (PURLS), so they can feel like you crafted something custom just for them.

Parthivshah.eLaunchers.com is an example of a personalized URL. It has a message specifically geared toward Parthiv Shah. You can build a personalized URL using wild card subdomains and AGS technologies; it is not very difficult to do. You also want to have a telephone number, so someone can call.

Okay, let's go back to the relationship between two humans. When you approach someone and they smile at you or they give you a signal that they are ready to have a longer conversation, what are you supposed to do? You are supposed to make a move right away without hesitation. Because if you don't make your move, if you ignore them, what happens?

They will move on; you will move on, and nothing good or rewarding will happen. That's why it is so important to respond when they respond. Your marketing will work. Your marketing will make you attractive to a handful of people who want to have a conversation with you. When they respond, don't ignore them. Have your conversion theater or persuasion theater ready.

You also want to track and measure what is working, so you can turn off what is not working and turn up the heat on what is.

Develop measuring devices and a rubric of success, your definition of success. You want to define clearly what you consider working and what you consider not working. You should constantly measure the efficacy of your marketing campaign. Be sure, when you are orchestrating your approach, you have your measuring devices, your response mechanism, and your multiple streams of response capture method ready. Also, be prepared to have the next phase of communication. This is what we call the respondent communication mechanism. You want to have respondent communications material at-the-ready, so you are sending information immediately to people who are requesting it. Be ready when they are ready. If you are not ready to mate, don't go on a play date. You don't want to disappoint someone, right?

Now that you are ready and now that your response receptacles are in position, let us talk about the last part of the orchestrating: the bait, the offer. Let's go back to the conversation we had about who you are, what you are, why you are, who you are for, how you want to please them, and if you have the capacity to please.

Go ahead and make an offer to please someone with no strings attached. If you are genuine and if your message is meaningful, you will be a welcome guest. So, be a nice human being; reach out and volunteer to help someone. Make a difference in someone's life. Make an offer. Make an irresistible offer: a book, a free report, a series of videos, or an informational single video. Think about giving them some piece of information that can change their life. It could be a secret: something you know and something they ought to know. Your marketing message is, "Hey, if you care to know about this, please allow me to share this with you; give me your name, email, and phone number, so I can share it with you."

We have a process called the two-step squeeze. On the landing page, you will basically have a squeeze with an offer. Please give us your name, email, and phone number, and we will give you this or that. Or, you can receive this special report, or you can watch this video—stuff like that. As soon as they give you their name, email, and phone number, you want to take them to a secondary squeeze where you can say, "Thank you for your request; here is the gift that I promised. Now if you give me your name and address, I want to ship you this box or package."

This converts them into a more qualified lead because they shared more information with you. They are telling you what they need; they are volunteering their information, and they are giving you a clear signal that they are waiting for your advice. Can you do this? Go ahead and make your approach.

CONSENT

Now that you know who you are, who you are for, how you want to please them, your market, message, media is figured out, and you have carefully crafted and executed your approach, consumers will either ignore you or respond to you. If they ignore you, reach out to them again, and again, and again, and again. Remember, you spent a lot of resources, time, and energy figuring out who you want to go after. Don't give up on them too quickly. People are busy. People want to know you want them.

It may take more than one or more than three or more than seven attempts to get their attention; keep at it. You want to chase them until you get their consent. How are they going to give you consent? They will raise their hand and say, "Yes, I am interested." Or, they are going completely ignore you or issue a cease and desist order.

If they are interested, they are going to buy something; they are going to make a phone call, and they are going to fax back a response. We spoke in the last chapter about response mechanisms. They will send you a reply card; they will send you an email; they will visit a landing page, or they will do something to say, "Yes, I am interested," or they won't. We're only interested in those that raised their hand. The remainder may not be ready now, but they might be down the line.

So what do you want to do about those who have come forward? You want to qualify the respondent.

There is a concept called the brain-dead offer. For example, I am a pen nut. I love buying Montblanc and Cartier pens. I have more than $20,000 worth of pens on my desk. Now, I am going to offer you a pen that retails for $500 for $75 or $50, you are probably going to say yes.

But what if you just don't like expensive pens? You will probably say "No" to this brain-dead offer. If this is the case, I should stop trying to sell you pens. You're not going to buy one no matter what. If my segmentation was pens, I do not have the capacity to please you in the way that you want to be pleased. Therefore, I should write you off, close your file, remove you from my database, and move on. There's no sense beating a dead horse.

When someone does give you consent, you want to acknowledge their consent and deliver to them what they asked for. Give them the gift that you promised. Then, ask them to either get more intimate by buying something, reading something, writing something, or giving you an appointment to come to an event. Find some way for them to engage with you in a meaningful way. You may or may not make any money. But, you gave it a try. Don't be disappointed; you made a friend, but they just aren't ready to deepen the relationship just yet.

Let us talk about the concept of SLO. The acronym SLO stands for self-liquidating offer. Send them a book, a DVD, and a whole bunch of information about the subject that you want to talk about, and tell them all they have to do is cover the cost of postage. What you are doing is signaling a potential buyer. The human, who has the capacity to take out a credit card and engage in a transaction, is a qualifier. You are identifying an interest.

They are not just saying, "Yeah, yeah, sure, send me your stuff." They are actually putting a couple of dollars on the table. That is called a buying signal. The concept here is a buyer is a buyer is a buyer is a buyer. When they buy, they are committing to a relationship.

If you don't get consent, you will not be able to go too far. The concept is to ascend an initial respondent into a small transaction; we call it a monkey's paw. In the concept of monkey's paw, what they say is "don't sell me the whole enchilada." Sell a little bit of something that can lead to a larger, more lucrative relationship. In general business terms, this is also referred to as a micro-commitment. How will you get them to buy something small, just to try you out? Dr. Charlie Martin calls this concept Experience the Genius.

Now let us talk about what I do. When a client wants to buy the services of eLaunchers, I essentially deploy this Business Kamasutra framework into a client's life. How does it work?

Well, you and I meet in my office in Germantown, Maryland for a day and a half. You stay over; we work for 14 hours, and we draw a mind map of what can and should be done for your business. We do a SWOT analysis. We identify who your market segment is. We watch some videos from Simon Sinek. We look at some marketing plans that I have done for other people in your industry.

Then, we look at marketing plans I have done for other people in other industries. We brainstorm, and we put together a game plan that is going to work for you. That's $X,XXX dollars.

Now, we just got you pregnant with an idea as to what can and should be done, and I am going to do all the work. For $YY,YYY dollars, my team will execute what I planned. Then, if you want an agency relationship where my team can be available to you and you have access to me and my time, I'll do a concepts and strategy meetings on a monthly basis. That is an additional $Z,ZZZ dollars a month. That does not include the cost of printing, mailing, postage, federal express charges, and other media expenses

There are several campaigns that I can unpack and deploy in your business. I would pick out a campaign that I have done for someone in your industry, in your genre, in your situation—something I already have ready to go. All I have to do is make a few tweaks. Instead of charging you X dollars, how about I give it to you for free? All you have to do is pay for printing, mailing, and postage? That allows me to do something to you before I ask you for your money.

That is how I convert a consent into a first date. You are seeing an insane value; I am telling you how much I normally charge, so you already know how much money I am going to get if this works out, and you are mentally prepared. You know that I am willing to do one campaign for you for free, but I am setting the stage, so you will continue to work with me month after month for a monthly campaign for $X,XXX a month. That is a brain-dead offer. I will do all the work; the only thing you are paying for is printing, mailing, and postage. The graphic design work, all the content development work, and setting up a landing page, connecting it to your Infusionsoft if you have it, setting up the email, creating follow-up sequences, writing the script for your staff to follow up on the lead– all are done at no charge.

That's how I take a consent and turn it into a deal.

Whenever I get a lead or whenever I meet someone for the first time, I say, "I have four gifts; would you allow me to give you four gifts?"

Gift number one, I will give you a squeeze page, so people can leave their name, email, and phone number in exchange for a free report.

Number two is create a tell-a-friend button that can go on your website. A tell-a-friend button is a very powerful technique. It allows your friend or a client to click on a button and tell a friend about who you are, what you do, and how well you do it, so you can connect them to your business.

My third gift is putting these two codes on your Facebook profile or business page, so not just the website, but your Facebook page can also be an interactive income-producing asset.

My fourth gift is going to be an appointment scheduler, so someone can click on a button on your website and request an appointment to spend time with you.

In addition to these four gifts, the biggest gift I will give you is that I will spend twenty minutes of my life just trying to figure out what it is that you need and how technology can help. You may or may not even be in the market; you may or may not have the money to be able to hire me; you may or may not be in the same business that typically hires me, but I would give you all these gifts just because you are interested in me.

Why am I doing this? By the time you have my gifts, I know who you are, whether or not we are meant to be together, who else is in your ecosystem, how well and how in general you work with people like me, and whether or not I want to work with you. It helps me decide if you are the kind of person I want to work with. This is my lead qualification process.

If after consuming my gift I feel that we are not meant to be together, I will go ahead and mark disqualified on your lead sheet. We will keep you on our long-term newsletter list and send you occasional emails. If you need help, I will help you, but you are not in the small pool of opportunities that I am chasing to convert into leads and deals. That's how I take a lead to the next level.

TRUST

You have the consent. Now that the person has agreed to have a conversation with you, your number one goal should be to establish know, like, and trust, or KLT, with that person. Remember, people buy from people they like, and people will like you if they can trust you. Everyone's definition of trust is different. You need to establish trust in a way that they find meaningful. What do you do to establish trust? What do you do to measure it? What do you do to manage trust? How do you monitor trust, and when can you monetize it?

I want to move to a view of trust that I think is different from just about everyone. Let's talk about the anatomy of trust. Trust is a very mathematical thing. In my personal opinion, trust is about 10 percent emotional and 90 percent mathematical—meaning it is data and information-driven.

Trust can be established by willingly, openly, and preemptively—with no strings attached—sharing relevant, meaningful, and important information. If you know something about someone or something and if you are willing to part with information that is of important to somebody, it will immediately establish a thin level of trust. Now remember, this has nothing to do with someone liking you. They might like you and not trust you–that happens–, but if they trust you, more than likely they will like you.

What can you do to establish trust? First, find out what kind of information they crave. You can tell by looking at the webpage they visited, the ad they responded to, the questions they asked on the first call, or the referral source from whom they were referred. Or just you point-blank ask them, what can I do to have you trust me? Because if they cannot trust you, any sort of relationship is simply not going to work. The first thing you would do to establish trust is share information.

Other things that you can do to preemptively establish trust is to build credibility in the relationship. You don't have to be a household name; you just have to be recommended by someone who they are willing to trust, such as a celebrity endorsement on your website, half a dozen videos of your customers who can vouch for your integrity, Google reviews, a book that you wrote that they can read, a position of bestselling author on Amazon.com, or the New York Times. It might be a speech you gave at an establishment that you recorded and placed on your website. It could be your blog or other material that you can write. It could be something that someone says about you—a peer to peer communication. These are all elements that can establish the first layer of trust.

Once the trust is established during the dating period, you want to focus on elevating that level of trust.

How can you measure trust? Okay, if they trust you, they will share meaningful information. We are talking about information that can help seal your deal. You need to be asking the questions to evaluate your level of trust. Some of the questions I ask are, *"Who are you working with? Who is currently taking care of you? Am I competitive? Are you going to need someone else? Have you received other bids from other people? Can I look at them? Can I talk to other vendors that you are speaking with? Who else is involved in making a decision? Are you the sole decision maker? Can I talk to your partners? Is there anything else you want to see or hear before we get started?"* You want to ask questions. Your goal should be to get them to lower their guard and accept you as a professional. Just be careful to not sound like you are pressuring them for any of the answers. Make it a casual conversation.

Next, let us talk about monetary trust. Levels of trust can go up and down, and when levels of trust are down, there will be turbulence in the relationship. This is true in any relationship: a relationship between two businesses, two JV partners, a business and consumer, or even just two people in general.

How do you monitor trust? Trust is monitored by the information that you send out to see whether or not they are consuming that information. If they are not consuming your information, they probably wrote you off. It's over, and you just don't know it. You want to have interactive marketing material that they need to be actively involved with, for example surveys or quizzes.

You could ask them to watch a video and monitor whether or not they watched it or if they watched it in entirety. I have a friend of mine who owns a software company called Dilogr. This software allows you to place a video on your website, pause it on minute three, and ask a question. If the consumer says yes or no, you can play the yes video or the no video; it is called video piping.

The technology has advanced quite a bit. You can now ask them to download your iPad App, and you can track where they bookmark your stuff. I had a client who was a residential home builder, and we had an application for him. When someone goes to the builder's website, they have to register, and they have to log in. Once they log in, they can click on whatever home elevation they want to click, and they can select their options. The profile is savable and can be retrieved at any time. After spending 20 to 30 minutes on the website, when the family shows up at the home, the realtor just has to download their profile and say, *"I want to make sure; it looks like you prefer granite countertops."* This jumpstarts a conversations and can elevate trust.

It's a conversation about likes and preferences, and it shows a level of trust because they must have found the software interesting. We are already engaged in a relationship, and we can take the next step.

Let's talk a little more about the monetization of trust. You don't want to be too quick to ask for an order. If you try to monetize a relationship before the trust levels have solidified, it can backfire, and that might break the trust. Do what you can afford to do to establish trust; then, make an attempt to make a deal. If they are in the market and if they have to write a check somewhere, they will have to trust somebody.

Let us move to the role of data in the trust sphere.

In today's economy, information is everywhere. It is accessible in the most meaningful and the most analyzed way, and that is what is expected from you. People want information now—in the way they want it; that is what they are used to. That is the benchmark that is established by today's economy.

Therefore, you as a business have an obligation to understand how your customers and prospects capture, analyze, understand, read, and respond to data. That means you are going to have to build your information network— your digital nerve system, as Bill Gates calls it in his book *Business @ the Speed of Thought*. That captures information, catalogues it, analyzes it, and displays it in a meaningful way that establishes trust.

Not only do you want to display information, but you also want to monitor the consumption of the information that you are displaying. You want to monitor the consumption of the information that you are displaying; you want to ask for feedback and ask questions. You want to compute the information you are capturing in real time, analyze it, and reply to whatever your respondent is giving you.

If you take your eye off this ball, you lose. On arrival, you will not be able to establish a business relationship if you don't convince your prospect that you have taken time to listen to them and understand them. So, how do you establish trust when you are in a one-on-one meeting?

Make eye contact; look at them; don't do other things; ask permission to take notes; show them that you are taking notes. I use a software called One Note, from Microsft®. I also use my ImJet® and iMindmap® for mind-mapping, when I am taking meta-cognitive notes.

If you are having multiple conversations, I would begin mind-mapping the discussion, and I would generate a PDF of the mind map to send to someone and say, "Here's what I think we talked about. Please read this, and tell me if I missed something." If someone says, "Oh that argument should have been on the left-hand side note, not on the right side" or "Why did you do that in blue, that should have been purple?" Now, I know that I am being heard. Now, I know that we are on the same page.

Trust is not magic. There is no voodoo. You have to know who you are, who you are for, and how you want to please them. You must understand and find out if they want to be pleased that way. You need to organize, orchestrate, and execute an approach; get consent; and have them take the next step. Then you can begin a relationship and share data in a meaningful way. It takes all this to establish trust, and you are going to need all of this—in this order—to take the next step.

FOREPLAY

You have established trust. Now, they know you; they like you, and they trust you. You know who you are, what you are, where you are, and why you are. You know who you are for and how you want to please them. You have the capacity to please them. You have identified who you want to please. You have decided how you want to please them, and you have approached them.

They have given you consent to get to know you better. You have established a trust, and you have built a rapport. You have elevated the trust to a level where they are giving you a consent for intimacy. They are ready to mate.

Think about that for several moments. Think about it long and hard. Mark this page and close the book, so you can concentrate.

Where is your head? Where is your heart? You are in front of the person you really want to be with, and you are about to do what you are meant to do. But before you start mating, consider both your mindset and theirs. Are they as happy as you are? That's the concept of foreplay, making the other party as happy as you are about mating.

What would you do to make the experience more pleasurable? What about foreplay and some techniques to enhance it. What does McDonald's do to please you about the food they serve (healthy or unhealthy, that does not matter)? They have happy meals, right? They say with a smile, "Would you like fries with that?"

Delta Airlines gives reclining seats, in-flight entertainment, alcohol, and the Delta lounge. Marriott provides free apples in the lobby, cookies at night, and fruit-flavored water in the lobby so you can hydrate yourself on arrival. What does Disney do?

What do you do? What do you do to induce happiness in someone's life?

If you have ever been to Dr. Charlie Martin's office in Richmond, VA, you cannot tell that you're in a dental office—there is a baby grand piano in the lobby. There's a little internet café, so you can work while you wait; paintings on the walls; and a calming, soothing, and welcoming atmosphere before you are admitted.

I visited an orthodontist in Pennsylvania, my private client, Dr. Jason Hartman. His building was featured in *Today's Orthodontist* for the modern looks and how they are presenting their office. They actually bought a building that was an old bank, and it's really cool. They took the whole drive-through area and enclosed it. That's their treatment area. There is a huge bank vault in the office. Inside the safe sits their marketing department.

Get a tour of the facility, and you want to send your child there. The is ultramodern equipment. A high ceiling gives you a sense of wide-open space. The office is also a well-lit environment. It even has a brushing area where kids can brush their teeth before they start treatment.

If you have been to Dr. Dustin Burleson's office, there is a special area for VIP patients, with a refrigerator. They don't have a receptionist. They just have a patient lounge off the foyer with a greeter who welcomes you. This kind and lovely person invites you into the lounge to be comfortable. But, you are free to wander around in the room at your leisure. There are video games for the kids and a couple of computers for parents to do their work if they want. People can read or watch TV, watch a video on a tablet, and a host of other activities.

What can you do to engage in foreplay before you mate? Here is one thing that everyone would get aroused with: information. You should tell them something that calms their fear and establishes rules of engagement. It should give them consistency on the delivery. Multibillion-dollar franchises like McDonald's and Burger King have standardization and systematization, so they can provide consistent mediocrity, and this consistent mediocrity is acceptable.

As a matter of fact, consistent mediocrity is so powerful that if you are in a foreign land, you will probably pull into McDonald's because they will be open, you will get your sugar, you will get your fat, you will get a well-lit environment, and you will get a smile. And, there will be a clean bathroom where you don't need permission and a key to use it. They have established themselves. They have established rules of engagement based on consistent mediocrity. They still manage to surprise you: service with a smile—usually—a toy with a happy meal, packaging, and white-colored paper to wrap your food in. They consistently have a reasonably clean environment with visibly accessible condiments. These are all things that McDonald's and Burger King use for foreplay.

Here is a framework for foreplay-style education. You want to start with stating the problem. What is a problem, why is it a problem, is it worth solving?

You want to talk about the consequences of not solving it. What happens if it gets ignored? What happens when the problem gets worse? What happens when it is solved?

Now that you have invested in solving the problem, you give them what you have offered. You will tell them what you hope will happen, what the complications could be, and what the most likely scenario will be.

You also need to discuss, what you don't want to see happen, what you want to see happen, and what the rules of engagement are. Then you need to ask them "Are you okay? Are you ready to play?"

Then assure them that you are the right guy for the job. Ask them if they are sure they want to go through with the treatment? In Sandler, they call it post-fill or take-away. Give the human option to back away—it's the one fundamentally powerful thing you can do.

Show the guarantee; show the risk of not doing it, and tell them that if God forbid this does not work out, you always have an option to exercise their money-back guarantee.

Remind them that they are to ignore this situation and eliminate that fear; then, induce anticipation of pleasure.

Here is another very powerful thing that is a sure-fire way to establishing foreplay and creating an anticipation of pleasure: watch other people in the act (okay, keep your mind on what we're really talking about). It could be videos, pictures, words, testimonials, video testimonials, or pictures of you with one or two of your clients. How about pictures with you and celebrities, pictures with you and your family? Perhaps pictures of them and their family or colleagues interacting with you? What about pictures of you and your staff working on other people?

This prepares them to interact with you even when they are not with you, even when they are just thinking about you.

It is a visual artifact, videos, imaging, or text that facilitates fantasizing about doing business with you—that is going to induce foreplay.

The purpose of foreplay is to anticipate mating and have the pleasure of that anticipation. Organize a meeting, buy an info product, go to a healing session, go to a college, write a book, take a call—no matter how dull, boring, mundane, or dry your business is, it is my business.

I do marketing automation and implementation of Infusionsoft; I build WordPress sites and design marketing material. I analyze data for living; I do math.

There isn't anything cool, awesome, wonderful, sexy, or pleasurable about it—until you make money, of course. That gets people excited, but up until that, the process of doing the whole thing can be like delivering a baby.

If you are talking about harvesting all your material from everywhere, putting it in one chronology, building your choreography, and putting together a game plan, a marketing plan, and a data plan, it's a lot of work. It is about 50 to 75 hours of work for me. It is about another 500 to 600 hours of work for my team, so that is work on your part. If you want to do stuff, you have to pay me.

I don't do everything that you need. I don't write copy. I don't do search engine optimization. I don't do Facebook advertising. I don't do social media, and we have limited graphic design capacity. So, we'll be bringing in a couple of other vendors to do a few other things. I don't do animated videos; I bring someone in for that. There will be a half-dozen other affiliated suppliers that I will be bringing in, and you will work with them a little bit as well.

How do I make that experience pleasurable? One, I make it a point to tell the client that I am with you all the way. My main goal is to do whatever it takes to make you money. I will show competence; you are not my first client, and you are not going to be my last client. About 99 percent of the time, I am not learning something new from you. I am practicing my trade, and you are my bread and butter client. That makes you confident, that makes you happy.

I am telling you that there are 2,000 things to be done that you now no longer have to do because you wrote a check. Now somebody else is responsible, and that should get you excited.

Sometimes things go wrong. We are all humans. My business is the "people doing things" business. We DO stuff. Sometimes, humans make mistakes. Sometimes someone forgets to do something. When that happens, you can apologize, promise to do good, and make it up to them; you need to make a sincere attempt to undo the wrong you may have done. Not only will they forgive you, they will admire you for the way you have handled a lousy situation. But people will never, ever forget how you made them feel.

So, now that you know who are, who you are for, how you want to please them, and that you have the capacity to please them. They want to be pleased; they have indicated that they want to date you; you have been dating; you have established like and trust, and you have consent for intimacy. You are getting ready to make the deal, so how do you want them to feel?

MATE

Here we are, we're ready to play. You know why you are, what you are, who you are, who you are for, how you want to please them, and you have the capacity to please them. They want to be pleased the way you want to please them, and you are willing to accept what you get in exchange. They have said "yes." They have indicated an interest; they have been dating you; you have established trust. You have elevated the trust; you have engaged in some foreplay; you have established an environment where they are anticipating engaging in a relationship with you. They are ready. You are ready.

Now about the mating: Do you have the capacity to mate? Are you for real? Does your deliverable have potency? Will it do for the client what you promised? Are you good at what you do? Are you better than your competitor? Are you at least good as you say you are?

Because if not, at the moment of truth, facts will prevail. You don't want to disappoint someone after foreplay. That shatters trust. That breaks relationships. That breaks hearts. You cannot cure a broken heart. Oh, sure, you can apologize. You can ask for forgiveness. You can have them work with somebody else and pay for it. You can give them their money back, but you will never get them as excited as they were before you broke their heart. The relationship will never be the same. So don't pick a battle that you don't have an ability to win.

There are millions of ways to make money. Do what God intended you to do. There is a market for that. But after all the foreplay, potency, and mating, it is the most critical thing that you can offer. As a matter of fact, your ability to mate is a foregone conclusion and a belief on which Business Kamasutra framework is built. If you aren't no good, please put this book down; put it in an envelope; send it back to me, and I will send your money back. This framework is not for you.

You will not be able to afford to spend the amount of money, time, energy, and resources to do everything else that leads up to mating if you don't have the capacity to mate. Imagine, a plane runs out of fuel, so you have to get out of the plane. Imagine the hotel room is not clean. Imagine the plate or cup at the restaurant not being clean. Does any of that happen to you at the Marriott? At Delta? We're human, and we all have bad days. That's okay. Shit happens. There is no denying that. You will always have situations where things did not go the way you intended or wanted.

Physicians have complications. It could be so bad that they could lose a patient. Inadvertently, you could do a lousy job for a patient. You may make an error in judgment; you could forget to do something; you will screw something up.

A vendor will do something that was less than perfect, and you don't have time to do it over. What do you do? It's time to face the music, time to engage the client in solving the problem.

There is one way to handle it, there is one asset you have that will always come in handy. If something bad happens, when a deal is going sideways, when things are not going your way, when you are losing money, you always have one friend that you can depend on: your checkbook. You can spend your way out of almost any misery because here is what happens when you take out your checkbook.

First, you have acknowledged that you have a problem and told the client that you have a problem, and you are taking out your checkbook. You now have your client's undivided attention. The client knows that we have a problem, and they need to participate in solving it.

There is no negotiating or pointing fingers; everyone is in a position to get out of this mess as fast as possible. So the focus is on speed, and the focus is on getting out of this turbulent environment. A new enthusiasm is infused into the scene. You have time and money to do what you want. With money, you can buy resources you originally could not buy. You can hire new people; you can bring in new subject matter experts.

When I have something bad happen, let's say on Infusionsoft or WordPress technology or even direct mail, I can call Infusionsoft experts, and there are 250 of them available. I merely have to say "Hey I have a problem. This is my client; this is what I intended to do; this is what I have done. It ain't working; what do I do? Can you give me your opinion? Now that I have your opinion, how much would you charge? Don't save me money; make me look good. Tell the client that I am committed to solving the problem."

I had that happen at a law firm that I took on to do this Business Kamasutra framework. The guy flew in to meet with me; we put together a fulfilled marketing program, and we failed at the whole thing.

Because I cannot write copy, I hired a writer who was supposed to be a good writer, and he took the money. Then he did a slipshod job. I don't know how to write copy. I don't know how to tell what bad copy looks like. I did now know what we were looking at, and it was not until really late in the game that we realized it was a slipshod, really lousy project. It was so bad that I broke his heart, I lost his trust.

Back then, I did not even have the fiscal resources to give him his money back. He told me, "Parthiv, I want to walk away from you. I will let you keep $10,000; give me the rest of my money back." The rest of his money was gone. Everything we paid to the external vendors, to the other team members that I pulled in, and to the copywriter who charged somewhere between $20,000 to $30,000.

Back then I was so poor, I did not even have the money to take care of him. I gave the client two options: You can walk away from me with me owing you money and making a payment plan or you can find a vendor of your choice and let me pay the bill.

Together we found a vendor, and I had a heart-to-heart with him. I said, "Look, man, this is the situation. I did not pick you, the client picked you. They are comfortable with you. I am not going to ask you for a discount, and I am not going to ask you for a payment plan. All I want is you to save my ass. I want you to save my reputation. I want you to take care of me and make the client happy. I don't want the client back; I don't think I will ever get him back anyway. I don't expect the client to fall in love with me again. But please restore the trust; have the client respect me. I don't want his testimonial for my website. I don't care if he does not write me a good review. I don't deserve that. I hurt him; I took his money and did not deliver what I promised. I deserve to lose that relationship, but please do everything for him, so he is no longer mad at me."

That's how you mate. If you don't have what it takes to please your constituent in the way that they want to be pleased, don't engage in a relationship or end up doing something everything you have to do. Don't take somebody's money and run. Don't break their heart. Don't disappoint someone; if you disappoint someone, at least stick around until you are excused, until they say, "It's okay, let us move on." If you can do that, there won't be any disputes because everyone wants to win—even if they have to manufacture a win-win.

RELATIONSHIP TRANSFORMATION

Let's assume you had your first transaction with your client. Congratulations. I hope it was as enjoyable for you as it was for the client. I hope it was profitable. I hope it is the beginning of a brand-new relationship. In this chapter, let us examine what happened and what happens next.

The first transaction is important because that gets you in a role where the person is getting accustomed to intimacy with you. You have spent an awful lot of effort identifying who you are, what you are, why you are, and who you are for. You've toiled learning how you want to please and how they wish to be pleased. Do you have the capacity to please them that way and are you prepared to accept what it is that they are willing to offer in exchange?

You have organized, orchestrated, and executed an approach; they gave you consent. You took the consent and established trust. You've elevated the trust, and at the right time you monetized that trust. This was no accident. You were meant to be together.

They are also as anxious to do more with you as you are with them. So, while you are in the mating period, you want to establish the rules of engagement to engage in a lifelong relationship.

Now, this is up to you; it is not up to them. You do not want to offer them a buffet of services to pick from; you want to take your entire offer and create a choreography as to what comes next. Yes, you need to tweak the choreography based on what they need, but you want to have a predefined path in the relationship. This is called an ascension ladder. When I draw my ascension ladder, I do not draw a straight line up, going vertically from bottom to top.

I draw a curve that goes from left to right and bottom to top with ascension points all along the curve. Why do I do that? Well, because the ascension happens over time— you cannot rush it. If you push too hard, the client will feel the pressure, and you will feel resistance. However, the ascension ladder needs to be visible; because if they want to move faster, you do not resist– you let them soar. You let them rise as close to you as they are willing to pay. Let's look at some of the ascension ladders.

At eLaunchers.com, our ascension ladder, my ladder, is different, like I said previously. How do we begin our relationship? You would start with a free report—the success blueprint on my website. As soon as you request it, I am going to take you to a thank you page. You are going to receive your digital copy of the blueprint, and then I am going to say, "I have a couple dozen mind maps of my notes along with some workbooks. I have a marketing planner, a printed copy of the blue book, and maybe a copy of Business Kamasutra. Or maybe just a chapter or two from Business Kamasutra."

I might offer a book from Dan Kennedy, or whatever gift that I wish to give you. I'll suggest that if you give me your name and address we will ship you these gifts. Another way to do that is to say, "Oh, I'll ship you all those gifts, but just cover the cost of shipping and handling, and pay $5." It's called a self-liquidating offer.

The next step is a 20-minute consultation where you are going to meet with me. I get to meet you. I get to ask you who you are, what you are, and why you are. In my mind, I want to figure out if we are meant to be together and whether or not I would like you to be on my ascension ladder.

It would be nice to have your money, but yours isn't exactly free money—I have to work for it. If I have to work for it, I will make sure that I will be successful. I'll make certain that I have the capacity to please you in the manner that you want to be pleased. I'm also going to ensure that you are not going to annoy me. You are going to follow my process, and you are going to allow me to practice my trade. If you do not let me work the way I normally work, then it is going to be resistance all the way. I do what I do in an environment that I find conducive. I want to make sure that

I will get that if we are going to do business together. Then I will give you my four gifts, and by the time you consume my four gifts, I would have installed some software codes in your website and your life, which will give me a better look at your technical landscape. Then, I will mostly likely have the ability to understand your win condition, what makes you pleased, and if I have the capacity to please you that way.

Now that we are at that stage, we have a program called a free campaign. This is where we would look for a market segment and put together a brain-dead offer to signal buyers. Maybe it's a free report, a digital gift, a physical gift, and—if you have Infusionsoft—a three to five-step email campaign. We do all of that for you—for free; it costs me $800 to actually do the free gift. Why would I do that? Well, if you do not buy when we meet for the first time, we will have to chase you. Chasing you means we will have to call you; we will have to meet you; we will have to put you on a long-term nurture campaign.

All of that takes time, energy, resources, and money. If I spend all that money that I have earmarked to convert an opportunity into a deal and to bring something for you, most people will accept the deal. This gives me a chance to test the theory that my process will in fact work, and that I actually do have a capacity to make you money. We'll see if the free experiment works and if I can get you some customers before I take your money. If you are not going to buy after that, I should move on. That is my definition of what we call "experience the genius"—a free campaign. Sometimes, a free campaign may not be the most appropriate step; you might want to come in for a day-long consultation, or you might want one of the other packages. Those again all come with a money-back guarantee. If things don't work out, I am risking very little money—I am not putting my life on the line for a $30,000, $40,000, or $50,000 project backed by a money-back guarantee. I am putting my neck on the line for a $4,000 to $5,000 package. That risk is affordable, as I am testing the relationship with you.

The next step would be an initial consultation followed by a full marketing makeover. The initial consultation is a day-and-a-half affair where you come to Germantown, MD. We look at other peoples' mindmaps that I have built. We will look at some business concepts and technology workflows that have been deployed for other people, which have been successful. We will look at your situation and see what fits, and we will put together a mindmap of what needs to be done. We'll determine what can and should be done. We will do a SWOT analysis to identify your strengths and your weaknesses, and we will put together a mechanism to identify opportunities where your strengths are relevant and your weaknesses do not matter. That way, we can look for some low-hanging fruits in your life that we can chase in round one. I usually look for a good $40,000, $50,000, or $60,000 worth of a new business that can be generated for you in round one. Most businesses who do $500,000 to $2,000,000 in revenue usually have that kind of money just kicking around in their business, which nobody has pursued—lost opportunities, unconverted leads, an ascension that you have never approached, or something along those lines.

So, there is always money to be made in everyone's life. I just look for that opportunity during the initial consultation. If I cannot, then it is not going to work out. My process is not magic. I cannot make money appear out of nowhere, so I give them their money back, reimburse their airfare and hotel, and give them a ride home. I chalk it up saying I made a friend out of it, and it only cost me a couple of bucks.

But if all goes as forecasted, it's another story. As soon as we begin working on the marketing makeover, another thing that I encourage my client to sign on to my monthly marketing managed-care services. That runs anywhere from $2,500 to $7,000 a month. It gives you the luxury of having me and my entire team becoming your marketing department, so you will never have a lack of resources. You can do whatever the hell you want to do, when you want to do it.

Oh, you want to exhibit at such and such event? Done. All the pre-event research is done. The marketing plan is developed. We now buy the list of attendee leads, send out a three-step direct mail campaign, and have consumers preregister on the landing page so they can RSVP to come and meet with you. We'll have them preregister to meet you at the booth. You will have a gift waiting for them. We can begin having conversations with them before you go to the show, and you can meet with them while you are there. We will have a special gift or prize that people can win. If they stop by your booth, a lead follow-up system is in place. You would scan the business cards of anyone who stops by the booth, and the data would be entered in your Infusionsoft account. Email sequences would go out to persuade them to schedule an appointment and bring them into your selling cycle.

This is just one campaign. We have about 50 of these campaigns that are pre-thought-out or done for someone else, which we can unpack depending on the opportunity that you want to pursue or threat you want to respond to.

There you have it; this is my ascension ladder. This is what we do at eLaunchers. If all goes well, I can convert an introduction or a referral into a multiyear, six-figure relationship. Why would someone get into a multiyear, six-figure relationship? Well, I look for two milestones.

One, sell enough of their services to pay for the money they invest. Let's say you spent $6,000 on diamonds in your database (missed opportunities as was explained earlier). My goal one would be to sell $6,000 in services, so you get the money you paid me from your own ecosystem, and you still have the assets of the campaigns we built.

My goal two is to make a three times return. You invested $6,000, and if we brought in $18,000, you paid for marketing, you made a contribution to your overhead, you moved some inventory, and you made some profit. We now have a reasonable assurance that we would be able to make money together.

Finally, I pledge to work until those two goals are met, and that is how the relationship starts in essence.

Why ascension is important? Well, it is important for several reasons.

First, you make your money when someone ascends. The entire Business Kamasutra framework requires a very well-thought-out, well-choreographed sales cycle that would require a highly-qualified prospect to follow your system. You cannot afford to do all that if all you are doing is a single transaction.

If you are a single transaction company, you may or may not be able to afford the true Business Kamasutra framework. You need to have an ascension ladder to sell them something else.

Second, one who is ascending is not leaving. Ascension is the best form of retention. A regular-paying client or customer is not going to easily give up on you and head somewhere else.

Third, the thought of a continuity activity will keep you in the relationship. Continuity income has a couple of very useful and valuable benefits. One, there is a consistent, steady stream of income that you can depend on and use to make infrastructural investments in your business. Two, the person who is paying you every month, even if it is $100, $200, or $500 a month, is in the business of giving you money. Whenever they have an opportunity in their life that they want to pursue or a threat that they want to respond to—if they are spending money on you—you will be their default choice to engage. You already have some of their money, so you will be asked to come into their new idea and hit the ground running.

This chapter is the entire Business Kamasutra framework. By drawing a relationship between how two humans mate and how a relationship with a consumer or a business builds, I am trying to streamline a standardized approach that every business can use to engage with their prospects.

In the following chapter, we will talk about truth of trade– what can you do, what tools are available to you, what technologies we use and you could use too, and what we have done. Over the course of several years, these chapters will change because by Business Kamasutra is a timeless principle of developing relationships between you and your prospects and customers, you and your joint venture partners. Truths of the trade will change, but the principles are steadfast.

In this version of the book we will talk about tools that are known to me as this book is written. So, you might want to visit the Business Kamasutra book website, download the latest version of it, look at the Kamasutra tool kit, and look at what tools, techniques, technologies, and processes that we have in process. We, and you, are always learning.

THE TOOLS OF THE TRADE

Now that you have drawn the parallels between relationships among two humans and relationships among businesses and customers, there are certain specific tools that can be used to facilitate each stage of the Business Kamasutra framework. Business Kamasutra is a framework, a workflow, and a standardized, systematized, documented business process that can be outsourced and automated. That is, if you are using standardized tools and a systematized workflow.

NOTE TAKING

The process that I use for meta-cognitive thinking is mind mapping. I use three software programs for this.

For a desktop, I use mindjet.com. I have a subscription to Mindjet cloud that allows me to store the maps in Mindjet cloud and open them on any device (phone, surface, desktop computer, someone else's computer, browser). It is an inexpensive tool that helps you think and draw a complex, multi-faceted, multiparadigm diagram and display it with ease.

I use three tools for three different purposes. When I am taking notes, I use Microsoft Onenote on my surface, and when I am using paper and pen I use pre-printed paper with Rocketbook. com grid, so I can scan from mobile to app and store them on OneNote. It helps me take notes in the order of the speaker speaking, and when the speaker jumps from topic to topic or takes me off on a tangent, I keep drawing what I hear. In a one-on-one session, it is easy for me to just show the map to the speaker and ask them to come back to the main topic.

When I am thinking, strategizing, or delivering a concept, I use iMindmap.com. I use colors to stay on course and make sure every argument stays within its role. The drawings are explosive—in absolute random order—as they come from my mind. These ideas have no concept of chronology, sequence, importance, weight, risk, cost, or time. What I draw on iMindmap.com are things that CAN AND SHOULD BE DONE. We don't know if we have time or money to do them, and we may not know what we will do first.

After that comes the Mindjet diagram. In Mindjet, I do not use colors. I simply use a CLOCKWISE diagram, which is a visual, sequential workflow of what I want done.

To draw a MAP, or marketing automation plan, I use a software called Gliffy (www.gliffy.com). Before the evolution of the campaign builder, Gliffy was the choice of strategists at Infusionsoft for drawing lifecycle marketing diagrams. I still do my strategy work on Gliffy. In addition to Gliffy, I have invested in other blueprint diagram applications, like Geru.com and a few others.

There are three other tools I used in the past for idea mapping. I used Balsamiq (on PC) or Omnigraffle (on Mac or iPad) to draw Infusionsoft funnel diagrams. I used these tools to communicate with my internal teams.

While I have access to all these tools, the best tool I have is my whiteboard. I have the entire wall in front of my desk painted with whiteboard paint, and I am always drawing on it. I draw; I take a picture of it with my iPad, and I add the picture to the client file. I record my notes using the voice recorder on my mobile phone and send the audio file for transcription. This way, I am recording all my notes and thoughts.

PROJECT PLANNING

We experimented with many tools, and after a lot of experimentation, we finally settled on <u>Monday.com</u>. We selected this tool because it has the functionalities of a Gnatt chart: resource allocation, project planning, budget management, and ability to integrate with QuickBooks and Infusionsoft. When you orchestrate a project, you will have three things to track: Milestones, Deliverables, and Tasks. We split things up into Milestones and Deliverables depending on what they are. Every milestone or deliverable has TASKS under them, and the tasks are assigned to the role-players. When the tasks are completed, the project manager will take the allegedly completed project and assign it to the QC team. Once the QC team performs end-to-end testing, the project is ready for client to approve.

WORK ORDERS: My project management team has developed editable PDF work orders that they share with vendors who are doing the work. We do all our technology development work, graphic design work, CRM implementation work, and web development work in house; we outsource certain items, such as print mail production and some specialized technology services. The work orders are released to the internal team and external vendors, who fulfill the work orders and report to the PMO (Project Management Office). The PMO accepts the work and orders the QA (Quality Assurance sequence).

QUALITY ASSURANCE: We have our most senior professionals dedicated to two things: WRITE WORK ORDERS and QC THE WORK DONE BY PRODUCTION TEAM.

The senior project leaders work with me and the client to discuss broad-stroke strategy statements and build work orders from the mindmaps and whiteboard drawings.

During the QC stage, they compare the completed work against the mindmap, whiteboard drawings, and broad stroke strategy to ensure that the finished deliverable in fact caters to the spirit of the original concept. ONE senior team leader or a member of the executive team, who is not involved in production or planning, is assigned to conduct end-to-end testing and experiences the campaign from the consumer's perspective.

We use a method called AUDIT. We have interns and trainees, who go through the exercise of developing various audits. We have a website audit, direct mail audit, Infusionsoft audit, and campaign audit. In audit, the intern or trainee would click on everything and write a screenshot by screenshot narrative of what happens when certain link is clicked. They dial the phone number; they visit the website or landing page; they fill out the form; they visit the thank you page, and they record a screenshot of every step. If anything is not working, they circle it in red. The audits go to the leadership team as a reference document. This is a crude internal memo-style Word document, and it is not necessarily suitable to share with the client, but sometimes clients are so involved in the project, they work off of the audit document too.

SEGMENTATION

There are three parts of segmentation, and different tools are used for different parts:

PART ONE is about YOU. It's when you define who you are, why you are, and what you do. It also speaks to what your company does for the world, who you want to please, how you want to please, and if you have a capacity to please.

You are going to be detecting this information from within. The amount of information you will find when you go soul searching can be overwhelming. You will need tools to capture information, catalog information, analyze it, and draw your picture in a meaningful way.

Analyzing what you see is at least as important as the paradigm you have. Unanalyzed data is just noise. It exists; it buzzes around you; it does not do anything for you, and it gives birth to chaos. So, to go from chaos to clarity, you need to develop meta-cognitive thinking.

PART TWO of segmentation is about WHO YOU ARE FOR. This means who your prospects and customers are going to be, moving forward. Chances are, your current clients ARE your ideal clients. But we need to find that out first. This is done by first drawing a picture of your IDEAL CLIENT. We get as specific as we can get in terms of defining your ideal client. Techniques used for this are secondary research, comparative analysis, data analysis, and primary research.

The most potent tool I use for this exercise is COMMON SENSE. We just talk. We write down on the whiteboard what matters to you. If you are a successful business owner and you are going through this exercise, there is a lot of information up there in your head. We need to get that information out and put it on the analytics table. Your wisdom and your common sense paradigm is my PRIMARY gauge.

We also do comparative research. We study competition; we study similar businesses, who might be willing to share information. We look through my library of mindmaps to see what other people like you have done or said.

PART THREE of segmentation is HOW YOU WANT TO PLEASE. Here we are not just defining your product, but we are defining what problem your product will solve, why it is important, why it is worth solving, and who will ultimately benefit from it. It is a very humbling exercise.

This again is going to be a complex idea diagram, because you will be talking about the what, how, and why of your product offering. In this exercise you will also build your entry-level product (also referred to as "tripwire") and ascension ladder. Some consultants call the ascension ladder a "funnel." My friend Dustin Matthews is an expert at building funnels, and he uses a diagram that looks like a funnel. I prefer to use an ascension ladder. Either process can use Microsoft smart art to draw your diagram.

For list research, my favorite tool has been <u>SRDS.com</u>. I look for targeted buyer lists, composite lists, compiled lists, subscriber lists, and donor databases. For consumer demographics and psychographics, I have always used Acxiom and Experian. I access these files through a composite data consolidator called AccuData. For business to business lists, I have always used D&B.

We all have our favorites, and we develop our favorites based on our experience. Just because I name-drop my select few suppliers does not mean other suppliers in this space are not good. I may not have experience with them yet.

You can rent a mailing list, a telephone list, a fax broadcast list, and/or an email list. Keep in mind, however, that fax broadcast is illegal in most places.

However, it is important to note that there are significant regulations that play a role in telling you what you can and cannot do. There is a DO NOT CALL regulation that requires a telemarketing organization to acquire a SAN number before you start your telemarketing campaign or even get a copy of a telemarketing list. Consumer privacy regulations disallow certain types of intelligent data overlay. CAN SPAM regulation, usually interpreted and enforced by industry ASPs (application service providers), prohibits you from sending an email to a cold list.

How do you go about sending an email blast to a targeted list of PROSPECTS who did not give you consent to contact yet? First, you don't rent the list and import the data in your Infusionsoft That violates Infusionsoft's policies.

Almost all email deployment services will have similar policies prohibiting you from buying email lists and sending out broadcast messaging.

If you want to send an email to families who have donated $1,000 to your favorite charity, you would buy an insertion order from the charity. The charity will send out an endorsed email on your behalf from their email system. You are authorized to send follow-up email messages to people who RESPOND to your offer.

You might want to consider SPONSORING an email or a print newsletter that an association or organization sends out. If you want to reach pediatric nurses at home addresses in your local geographical area, a local association or a union of pediatric nurses would cheerfully include your sales letter or a postcard in their newsletter package if you pick up the tab on printing, mailing, and postage of their newsletter.

Now you arrive in THEIR envelope, ushered into a relationship. If you want to reach employees of companies within a three-mile radius of your business, you can come up with a BRAIN-DEAD OFFER, such as a corporate discount for employees of XYZ company, and reach out to the HR director of the company to seek permission to do a payroll stuffer or an employee break room poster.

Affinity marketing and a champion letter can be a very useful trick of the trade. You can pledge to donate a certain amount a sizable amount—as a match fund where the charity will send a donation appeal letter to their existing donor base with your story and your offer to match their donation. In exchange, the donor would make a connection with you, and you will be able to have a conversation about your services to the donor. I did a direct mail campaign for a food pantry in Boston that had no money to pay for printing, mailing, or postage. I approached a local bank who picked up the tab on the direct mail program, and the charity gave them a list of donors who responded to the offer. The bank matched the donations, minus the cost of direct mail, and sent out a thank you letter to the donors with a promotional offer from the bank.

Remember the formula: Who you are, who you are for, and how you want to please them. You can please someone and get consent to have a meaningful conversation by making a contribution to their favorite charity.

Another little-known segmentation strategy is called "out-of-place advertising." A good example of it would be to have a dentist set up an exhibit booth at a bridal expo to offer a smile consultation for brides. My friend Dr. Dustin Burleson spends about a million dollars a year in direct marketing, and he generously shares his TESTED, PROVEN, WORKING swipe file to his newsletter subscribers. Visit www.eLaunchers.com/start to request a two-month free trial to this newsletter. After we talk, if appropriate we will send you a complete strategy document on the bridal marketing campaign (or another campaign appropriate for you), along with a copy of artwork of the three-step direct mail. You'll also receive a copy of the landing page, a three-email follow-up sequence, free report that you can share with brides who show interest in your services, and a telephone script for your staff to follow. If you are an orthodontist, a pediatric dentist, or a general practice dentist, and want to try this concept, my team will turnkey implement this campaign for you AT NO CHARGE. All you have to do is call my office at 301.760.3953 or send an email to pshah@eLaunchers.com and request a FREE Bridal LOS implementation.

If you need to buy lists once in a while, you can request a research appointment with me by visiting my website and requesting a list research appointment.

APPROACH

There are three parts to approach: organize, orchestrate, and execute. As Steven Covey says, "You want to begin with the end in mind." The desired end goal of an APPROACH is a consent to date; in this case, getting your consumer to complete tripwire purchase or respond to campaign.

ORGANIZE: To organize an approach, I use Dan Kennedy's MMM Triangle. It is called Market-Message-Media. He explains this process in great detail in his book No BS Direct Marketing. You first want to identify the market you want to approach. This is not a general directional approach as to where your company is headed. Here we discuss exactly who we are going to target for THIS campaign. If you are a dentist, you might want to reach out to brides and offer them a smile makeover, or you might want to offer a free mouthguard to children who play contact sports in order to have the child come to your office for an initial visit.

Once the market and message are defined, we discuss media. My favorite media are targeted, multi-step, direct mail: EDDM, free-standing inserts, special magazine/print advertising, online advertising, Facebook advertising & email marketing. SEO, PPC, social media, and outdoor advertising are not my area of expertise.

Here's how you want to plan the approach. You want to start with a statement of goals. The statement of goals includes the number of desired leads, desired conversion rate, desired initial transactions, and value customers have for the life of their relationships. Keeping these numbers in mind, you will develop a budget. My rule of thumb for setting desired goals is a three times return. I want to establish two milestones. Milestone 1 is to sell enough products/services to equal the dollars spent on the campaign. Milestone 2 is to sell three times what we spent on the campaign. That way you cover the entire cost of the campaign, contributed to overhead expense, and brought some to the bottom line.

ORCHESTRATE: Once you organize your approach, it's time to orchestrate the approach. This is also referred to as "project planning." Orchestrating a direct marketing project is a complex micro-production with a lot of moving parts and a lot of details. If you do not have a dedicated individual with thorough understanding of all moving parts, you might want to outsource the orchestrating work to a company with experience in campaign administration.

EXECUTE: Now that you are ready to execute your multi-step, multi-media, direct marketing approach to your targeted customer, the select media could be direct mail, email, telephone marketing, Facebook advertising, and pay-perclick advertising. In direct mail, I prefer to use FIRST CLASS mail, with NO presort, large 9 x 12 envelopes and handwritten addresses. For larger marketing programs with bigger lists, I like to use a simple three-step direct mail program.

Step 1 would be a letter with a BRAIN-DEAD OFFER and a CALL TO ACTION. The idea is to take them from offline to online and back to offline to obtain consent and start a conversation. We have a huge swipe file of thousands of direct mail campaigns we have done. You can request a sample campaign from our swipe library. Just reach the office at 301.760.3953 or email me directly at pshah@ eLaunchers.com to request a telephone consultation. I will review your situation and look for the most appropriate campaign sample I can send you based on your segmentation.

In direct mail production, my select vehicle is digital color printing facilitated by VDP (Variable Data Printing). I engineer the mail pieces using layered content overlay. I would have a layer of core content. Above that, I would build a layer of customization (versioning) content, and above that, I would have the level of personalization. You can create multiple steps in a direct marketing campaign by switching out layers.

BRAIN-DEAD OFFER: This is one of my prized concepts.

I shared this concept with my friend Paul Tobey, and he actually wrote an entire book on the subject of brain-dead offers called *Brain Dead Offer*. You can get this book on Amazon.com. This book dives deep into this concept. I have won many battles with this concept.

The concept is that a brain-dead offer should self-disqualify an uninterested prospect, so you stop wasting your time. Here's an example I use to describe the concept: I LOVE pens. I have a sizable collection of Montblanc and Cartier pens. I tell my clients that if I do something significant for them and go above and beyond the call of duty, they can reward me by sending a letter to my wife and request that she allows me to buy "one more pen." As I am writing this book, I have my eye on the 2014 Montblanc Gold Resin collection. So, here is a question for you: If I offered to sell you one of my pre-owned designer pens for $75, would you buy it? If you said NO, I should stop my follow-up sequence because you are just not a pen kind of a person. However, if you say yes, that does not mean you are a good prospect. We still don't know if you will buy it at full price, but we just made you an irresistible offer. I use this technique when I do not have a control vehicle in marketing. Almost always, I start my testing sequence with a brain-dead offer.

SLO (Self-Liquidating Offer): Once upon a time, there was this princess who was playing in the garden, and she saw this frog. She picked up this adorable little creature, who spoke to her sweetly. The Princess kissed him. Poof, the frog turned into Prince Charming and married the princess, and they lived happily ever after.

Now YOU are the princess; you are playing in the garden; you are looking at a whole bunch of frogs. But you just don't like the idea of kissing all the frogs in the garden just so you can find one Prince Charming. Sure, you'd like a Prince, but you are not kissing your way to finding one.

So, you are going to make an SLO (Self-Liquidating Offer). This is also referred to as a "tripwire." For a very small fee, just enough to cover the production expenses, you sell a small information product. It could be a binder, a DVD, an audio CD, a data CD, a workbook, or maybe a book for about $97. You are not going to get rich off of $97, but anyone who buys your SLO is a much better prospect. The purpose of the SLO is to signal a buyer. In some cases, I would take this concept further and develop an SLM (Self-Liquidating Membership) that keeps a prospect on a long-term nurture in the habit of paying money with you.

This book could have a membership site called Business Kamasutra Club. The membership can be $97 a month, and you accrue $97 a month in eLaunchers.com gift cards from day one. You can use the gift cards to pay for any consultation service at any time. Once you become a meaningful client of eLaunchers.com, you get a free lifetime access to the membership site and the newsletter—you just pay for printing and postage. This is a classic SLM. I don't really need $97, that's not the profit center or revenue model for me, but you are a lot more qualified prospect if you are a paying member of my club. (For a variety of reasons, we have decided NOT to have a PAID membership club like this as a companion to this book.)

CONSENT

If you know who you are, who you are for, and how you want to please them, and you approach them the right way with the right offer, they will give you consent to communicate with them. In direct marketing terms, this is called a "response", and the prospect is now called a "respondent".

Many businesses fail to make it easy for the prospect to respond. You want to have multiple channels of response vehicles: a dedicated phone number, fax back response, a business reply envelope (or a courtesy reply envelope), a landing page or a PURL (personalized URL), and a dedicated email address that captures responses and automatically responds to the respondents.

My choice tool for response capture, response management, and auto-response is Infusionsoft. I also love Hubspot and Active Campaign. There are other tools out there with similar functionality, and I am not making a claim that Infusionsoft is better. I am simply stating that my choice tool for this is Hubspot or Infusionsoft. I can use Infusionsoft to capture leads, set up SLO, set up SLM, collect money, and poll prospects, so I can send a relevant marketing message to the prospect based on what they are asking for.

What I like about Infusionsoft is it is not just a standalone application; it is an entire ecosystem made of consultants and certified partners like me. There are pre-built campaigns in a campaign library that you can swipe and deploy, an open API so we can push-pull data from almost anywhere, an open integration with Zapier, and dozens of applications that significantly enhance the functionality. What I like most is that all data stays in one place, in your Infusionsoft account, and all other applications use the data in the central data table. The record layout is simple, and you have an ability to add fields as necessary. The campaign builder can build web forms, order forms, and even Infusionsoft-hosted landing pages and shopping cart.

ESTABLISHING TRUST (DATE BEFORE YOU MATE)

Trust is a very mathematical thing. In my opinion, trust is about 10 percent emotions and about 90 percent math.

Because trust is mostly mathematical, you can use a mathematical algorithm to establish, manage, monitor, elevate, and monetize trust.

There are many ways to ESTABLISH trust. We will talk about a couple of things you can do to establish trust and rapport so you can start a conversation. An entire book is written by Dan Kennedy and Matt Zagula on the subject of trust, called Trust Based Marketing. Dr. Steven Covey wrote a book on the subject of trust called Speed of Trust. These book talk about proven formulas that help you establish and elevate trust.

You can buy these books from Amazon.com, or if you are a private client or a club member, you can call my office to request a copy of a book.

One thing you can do to establish trust is share meaningful information that they did not have. Most people think this is counterintuitive. Most people are secretive about their knowledge. Therefore, if you are willing to share what you know, especially knowledge that does not necessarily boast your own competencies that will establish trust.

Information like statistics, factoids, and anecdotal evidence may turn people off. The old-school, hyperbolic format of a free report might turn people off.

The free report should be written in the format of a white paper. It should be informative, educational, entertaining, and comprehensive. You cannot just open loops and not close them. Here is a persuasive gift-writing framework.

- Context and data around the problem
- Statement of problem
- The implications of this problem
- Why is it a problem

- If it gets worse
- If it is ignored
- What is the upside if we fix it
- Framing all the written material with "Common agreement" (Obviously…, clearly…, we all know… etc.)
- Proposed solution
- Based on the facts that are presented, I think we all agree that it is prudent to proceed in the following way…
- Statement of solution
- Identify how the solution will solve the problem
- Suggest alternative solutions if applicable
- Statement of risk
- Clear next steps

FOREPLAY

When you have elevated the trust to a point where they are ready to make a deal, you need to focus on pleasure and experience. There are two factors that will affect your ability to please.

First is knowing what pleases them. This goes back to who you are, what you do, what it does for your clients, and how valuable it is to your client. You want to start with their baseline expectations. What are they expecting? What will get them satisfied?

The concept of foreplay is to focus on exceeding expectations and setting yourself apart from your competition. What can you do for them that they are not expecting from you or your competition? Can you afford to do that, do it consistently, and show it off as a differentiator?

The following elements are likely to be well received for foreplay:

- Unannounced upgrades
- Speed—Can you do it faster?
- Accuracy
- Enhancement or bells and whistles that cannot be sold as an upgrade
- Chairside marketing material
- Testimonial booklets
- Educational videos displayed on a video book, preloaded iPod, or a private YouTube channel
- Book
- Implementation binder
- Infographics, Visual MAPs
- Large wallchart, mind maps
- Whiteboard drawings

BONUS SECTION: SEXY SIDE OF ROBOTICS

ESTABLISHING YOUR RHYTHM

If you think your business and its relationships with its customers, prospects, vendors, and partners has resemblance with the process of Business Kamasutra, you can establish and document your rhythm on how you will find business, close business, and grow business.

Why is establishing rhythm important? Because without rhythm you will be randomly doing things that may or may not be in alignment with your core values and your goals. You want to know who you are, who you are for, and what you will do to be in front of opportunities where winning will not be insignificant and losing will not be embarrassing.

For establishing the rhythm, we created an annual marketing calendar. It has a list of proposed daily, weekly, monthly, quarterly, and annual marketing activities. The calendar also has a marketing ROI calculator and a monthly marketing expense budget.

Working in a rhythm will also save you from the "shiny object syndrome."

So, how do you go about establishing your rhythm, and why don't you feel that you have a rhythm already established? Do you feel that you have a bunch of people living and working on an island, and they just do whatever they do, but there is no synchronization or harmony among them?

Fortunately, you are not alone. Most growing businesses have this problem. Some often refer to it as "growing pains," but in reality this is a problem that can be avoided or fixed.

Here is the root cause of the problem: Most businesses start with A HUMAN. The human buys or builds the apparatus that the human is comfortable or experienced with. As a business grows, the human brings more humans, and more humans bring more apparatuses that they are comfortable with. A growing business is a random collage of humans, apparatuses, processes, and silos of data. Eventually, everything gets out of hand, so the first human buys a management book or hires a management consultant, who comes in and tells you that everything you have ever done is WRONG and you have to start over and build a so-called "system".

There is a whole project management process that asks you to develop a stakeholder analysis, work breakdown structure, win conditions, and risk factors.

The problem with that line of thinking is that it is a bit too structured, too bureaucratic, too rigid, and it slows down the pace of a SMALL and GROWING business. You can't put a toddler in the military. A business needs to grow to a certain maturity before the "professional" project management and/ or process management systems can kick in and actually work. Therefore, for a successful, growing, SMALL business, you want a simplified version of process management. I call it RHYTHM.

Here's one way to build your RHYTHM without disrupting what you already have working. You first start with your MONEY line. How do you make money and how do you spend money (who pays whom, when, how, how much, how frequently & why).

Once you draw your money line, you will be able to build a database or a list of role players (or stakeholders). Segment the stakeholders into who takes money from you, who gives you money, and who are otherwise commercially important.

Once you have your stakeholders listed in these ways, you are ready to draw the data line. You can do this exercise with toy soldiers or Lego pieces or currency coins. Just put something on the table that gives you a visual.

You want to write down who consumes what data at what frequency and at what velocity before, during, and after the money exchange.

This will give you a very simple, basic data neurology. This basic data neurology can be used as a benchmark to build your DIGITAL NERVOUS SYSTEM for your business. You can read about this principle in Bill Gates' book Business @ The Speed of Thought. This book predates today's internet. This book gives you some "primitive" data intelligence concepts that are the foundation of how today's data scientists think, draw, write, and read.

This exercise will be easy, fun, and productive. Start with money, add humans to money, figure out how humans consume data and what VARIETY of data needs to be generated by what process in what VOLUME at what VELOCITY.

Once you have your three Vs of Big Data figured out, you build ONE central database that captures, warehouses, catalogs, analyzes, and displays the VOLUME and VARIETY of data at the VELOCITY that is meaningful to you and your ecosystem.

Once the central database is built, connect your current apparatus and your current humans to the new rhythm and train them.

If your business is at $500,000 to $2,000,000 in revenues, you might benefit from a workflow called "Magnetic Marketing Implementation A.B.C.D. (Any Business Can Do)." Please visit www.eLaunchers.com/start to download it or call my office to request a copy of this 32-page workbook. Be sure to ask for the companion USB Drive (or link to the vault) with my notes, mindmap, and a digital, fillable PDF of the book. This booklet has the same workflow at a much higher sophistication.

STANDARDIZE AND SYSTEMATIZE

Once you have your RHYTHM established, you can take steps to standardize your business processes, so you can systematize your business. Systematizing your business will give you something you may or may not have experienced: PEACE.

As the prime minister of India, Mr. Vajpayee once said in a speech, "Peace is necessary for prosperity." You will be more productive on a peace schedule compared to a war schedule.

So, how do you go about standardizing and systematizing your business?

For that, you need to find someone in your organization who has experience and understanding of business process engineering. This is something that comes to me naturally. PROCESS is my hobby. I enjoy observing humans at work, spotting their repetitive motions, and seeing if I can systematize it, so it can be automated, mechanized, delegated, or outsourced.

One day, I came back from an Infusionsoft conference all excited. I told my wife Dipa, "We are going to hire this company, who will give us a virtual assistant in the Philippines, at about $3 per hour, and our virtual assistant would be Infusionsoft trained. Just think of all the possibilities".

"OK," Dipa nodded. "Let's do this exercise. Why don't you pay ME $3 per hour for a few days. I will do exactly what you tell me to do. DO YOU KNOW WHAT YOU WANT ME TO DO FOR YOU?"

That's when it hit me! You cannot outsource unless you systematize. You cannot systematize unless you standardize.

In this chapter we will talk about the building blocks of standardization and systematization.

Here is the FIRST and most important rule:

In order to develop BUSINESS PROCESS AUTOMATION, you will need to first build BUSINESS PROCESSES. In order to build BUSINESS PROCESSES, you will need to build BUSINESS.

If you are not making money, spending money, and saving money you just don't have the necessary ingredients to build a standardized system. You HAVE TO make money.

Here is the advice I got from a friend when I started my business in 2002. All through my entrepreneurial life, this advice carried me.

"Focus on building a revenue stream. Start making money. When you have a deal in your hand and a check in the bank, the supply chain and affiliate network will form automatically. If you don't have adequate revenues, you will waste your time building your 'dream machine' and time will go by, and no one will buy anything, and you will eventually go broke and die hungry."

So, remember, it's okay to build a standardized system, but it should be built around your money line and your data lines, as discussed in the previous chapter about establishing your RHYTHM.

STANDARDIZATION: Standardization is also referred to as a "standard operating procedure" or a "process diagram." This is HOW things get done in your world.

Please take some time to OBSERVE and DOCUMENT how things get done in your world. Remember, just "observe and document." At this stage you don't want to judge or improve. You are not looking for excellence; you are looking for consistency. Consistent mediocrity is far more productive and profitable compared to an outburst of excellence followed by lackluster, slipshod, ambiguous, and undocumented mess.

Once you have documented the current state of your business procedures, you will be able to look for ways to improve your processes. You can document and improve your standards by identifying and eliminating unnecessary steps, circular workflows, and repetitive tasks. Most of the improvements will be quite visible, dramatic, and ultra-productive. Really small changes will yield measurable and impressive results.

SYSTEMETIZATION: Systematization is the process of tethering humans and apparatuses to your RHYTHM.

Once your processes are standardized by documenting and improving your processes, you can now draw up a systems diagram that would facilitate the flow of data through your digital nervous system. You can now tether your humans and their apparatuses to this data pipeline to build a system that can empower your entire business to work as one cohesive force and encourage cross-departmental data sharing. This will be a game changer. You will be able to see ACCOUNTING DATA for missed revenues. You will be able to see production data to be able to effectively buy resources just in time.

SYSTEM consists of a central database, a data neurology (also referred to as a digital nervous system), a system architecture that defines the role and flow of data between the stakeholders, a list of all stakeholders, standard apparatuses that are used by the humans, and rules of engagement among humans.

Let us describe each element of the System one at a time.

THE DATABASE: This is a central repository of information stored in ONE database or multiple RELATIONAL DATABASES that are connected to one another. Depending on your business, it might be unrealistic to build ONE database that would facilitate ALL the functionalities. I am not a big proponent of building a custom database solution for a particular business need. I prefer to find MULTIPLE off-the-shelf applications with complementing strengths and functionalities and build an API (application programming interface) bridge that would push/pull or synchronize data among multiple databases. Infusionsoft Marketplace has hundreds of APPS that connect Infusionsoft with other standalone applications making the 'ensemble' a complete information architecture. Salesforce. com has an ecosystem called APP EXCHANGE that connects the Salesforce.com CRM database to other applications in the cloud that perform functionalities that are not native to Salesforce. com.

THE SYSTEM ARCHITECTURE: This is a wiring diagram that would place various software applications in a compartmentalized chain. I built the Business Kamasutra System Architecture using Lego pieces. I have this toy on my desk. In the foundation, it has the Microsoft cloud computing platform or another appropriate cloud that will be home to all your data and applications. On top of the cloud. the platform is your brick-and-mortar business with all its processes that would make your business a "click-and-mortar business." On top of your click-and-mortar business is your FOUNDATION WEBSITE. Your website becomes the center of all business activities and the central hub of all online and offline communications for your business. In a following chapter we will talk more about the role of your website, the home page, the second squeeze page, interior pages, and destination page squeezes.

On top of your foundation website sits your business applications and databases. All of these applications, databases, foundation website, your click-and-mortar business, and your cloud computing environment are controlled by a CENT-COM command and control center that reports to a designated human.

DATA NEUROLOGY: This is the diagram that connects your central cloud computing environment, your click-and-mortar business, your foundation website, additional websites and microsites, business applications to the processing databases, and written rules of engagement between applications, processes, and humans on exactly how the data will flow between stakeholders and who will do what with that data.

APARATUSES: These are technical appliances like laptops, desktops, iPads, tablet computers, smartphones, paperwork for systems that use paper and pen for data capture, whiteboard diagrams, and other devices used by humans to access and control the system. Apparatuses are also used to view and consume data. When data is consumed properly, you will build a decision support system that is data-driven. This will give you a "data-vision" that will empower you to prepare for available opportunities and oncoming threats.

HUMANS: As described in the chapter RHYTHM, humans are the stakeholders or role-players. Humans are the consumers of analyzed data and generators of raw data. Without humans, the system has no purpose. Humans are also the most versatile part of any system. Whenever the system fails to capture, catalogue, analyze, or display information, humans can either play the role of the system or repair the system. Humans are also the weakest points of your system. Any system malfunction or underperformance of a system can probably be attributed to a human who did not do what they were supposed to do, or said human failed to use the system the way the system is designed. This is not a bad thing; it is a trait of the human as the role-player in the system, and this trait needs to be identified and compensated for.

Humans are the ONLY element of the system that have emotions. Emotions are qualitative data, which must be captured and quantified before being fed to the central database. The central database is essentially a reservoir of emotions between stimuli and response.

OVER-ENGINEERING: Yes, there is such a thing as over-engineering. Simplicity can be looked at in the following way: a person turns on a switch and a light bulb glows brightly. There is no thought to the process behind it and no multi-step process to go through. Many technologists have the tendency to build functionalities just because it is possible. Remember to split your needs between must-have and nice-to-have. I always tell my team members, vendors, and interns this simple formula: I will pay for it if it makes me money, saves me money, makes me look good, buys me more speed, buys me better accuracy, does something that is not getting done that should been getting done, or adds to my intellectual property.

Everything else is useless technology.

LET THE MACHINE DO IT

Marketing automation:

Once you standardize and systematize your sales lead generation, marketing, and sales lead conversion processes, you can in-fact automate it using off-the-shelf marketing automation tools.

There are many marketing automation tools on the market, and the Business Kamasutra Marketing Automation Workflow can be implemented using almost any off-the-shelf marketing automation software. My choice for this is Infusionsoft. It is my default choice for many reasons, however, I gravitate to Hubspot when appropriate.

I have been an application agnostic developer for many years. I have experience on working with CRMs like Microsoft Dynamics, Zoho, Act, Sage, Salesnet. com, Salesforce.com, Telemagic, Goldmine, and some homegrown systems in Microsoft Access and Filemaker Pro. For email marketing, I have worked on Exact Target, Vertical Response, Constant Contact, Mailer Mailer, Gold Lasso, MailChimp, and a few others. For e-commerce, I have used too many applications to mention. I have been building landing pages using HTML and SQL databases, and we have our own homegrown PURL engine that can generate personalized URLs. We have even created some advanced applications using my PURL engine and named them PURLIZED GURL and GURLIZED PURL. For marketing automation, I have worked on applications, such as A Weber, Office Autopilot, Exact Target, and a few others.

I am also a certified developer on multiple application platforms, and I have affiliate/reseller arrangement with almost all platforms.

So, holding other variables constant, why is Infusionsoft my primary choice? What is it about Infusionsoft that warms my heart?

A few factors:

1. It is the least expensive application in its class. For about $2,000—as an initial setup fee—and about three hundred dollars a month, you have an off-the-shelf application that becomes not only your marketing automation engine but also your primary data warehouse and data intelligence system. Sure, one can build a software from scratch with similar functionality but wouldn't that be over-engineering?

2. It is a SINGLE DATABASE with multi-faceted functionalities. It creates a record for each human in your system, connects your humans to the company they belong to, and keeps track of all touch points, all emotional interactions, and all fiscal interactions. It is a SINGLE DATABASE with CRM functionality, marketing automation functionality, lead capture functionality, e-commerce functionality, sales force automation functionality, and an email marketing system all-in-one.

3. It has an absolutely amazing network of consultants. The Infusionsoft consultants are called certified partners. I am a certified partner, and I have been part of the consultant community since 2009. The community of consultants is one large collaborative ecosystem. There is a culture of sharing and caring. Sure, there is an element of friendly competition, but frankly, there are just too many opportunities to make money in the community for anyone to engage in a fierce dogfight for a piece of business. On multiple occasions I have approached other consultants who are senior to me, and they cheerfully moved in and helped. On multiple occasions I have been approached by other consultants who are junior to me, and when they asked for help, we made our ecosystem available to them. Infusionsoft holds its consultants to really high standards, including a really tough initial exam, monthly continuing education credit requirements, and an annual recertification exam just to make sure you are technically competent to belong in the community. The community is small, elite, and affluent. It does not matter who you choose as your Infusionsoft consultant; you will be well taken care of. Anyone who has the CP badge is worthy of the price they charge. If they fumble, there are two hundred other consultants who will jump in and help out; all you have to do is ask for help!

4. An Open API with an ability to push/pull data from almost any ecosystem. Infusionsoft has a specific record layout that is adaptable to most business situations. In some situations where it is unreasonable to build a business application inside Infusionsoft as a native functionality, you can easily

build an external SQL data cooker that can take data from multiple sources and push/pull cooked data into Infusionsoft.

5. It has an intuitive and user-friendly interface. Okay, maybe I am pushing it a little bit. Infusionsoft is powerful, and with power comes complexity. It is not for the faint of heart. It does challenge the status quo. It requires a significant mindset shift for the business leadership team and a conceptual buy-in from your team members, but in reality, if this is how business is getting done and if you don't want to take the plunge, at least look at how your competition is going to kick your butt.

6. There probably is a precedence. Someone in your industry has probably done it before, and you can pick their brains on how they are using it. The culture of sharing information and tribal marketing goes beyond just consultants. I routinely introduce my clients to one another, so they can collaborate and learn from one another.

7. It integrates ALL channels of communications: email, letter, fax, voice broadcast, text messaging in an online and offline environment.

8. It tells humans what to do, and if humans do not do what they need to do, the system will keep reminding them until the human clicks on a button that "the call was made" or "gift was sent out."

Here is the Business Kamasutra campaign diagram. You CAN implement this yourself. As a matter of fact, if you reach out to my office and ask me for the Campaign Blueprint from my Infusionsoft, I will cheerfully give you the campaign blueprint, so you can implement the workflow yourself or hire a consultant to implement it for you. I will even provide guidance and advice to your selected consultant if invited to participate. As I said earlier, when I am not making money, I am making friends, and I need them both.

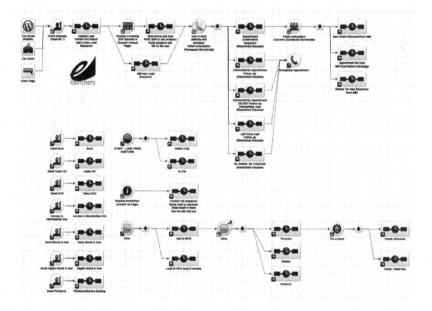

Let us look at various elements of the Business Kamasutra campaign and how it works.

1. **Lead Generation:** You will go through the segmentation and approach to generate QUALITY traffic to your website home page, a destination page, or a campaign-specific microsite or landing page. You can use WordPress to build your website and Leadpages.net or Optimize Press plugin for WordPress to build landing pages, thank you pages, and tell-a-friend pages. The Business Kamasutra Campaign has TWO web forms. One is called Initial Squeeze. This squeeze will capture NAME, EMAIL, and TELEPHONE NUMBER.

When you fill out your name, email, and telephone number, you are taken to a thank you page, which is in fact a second squeeze. On the second squeeze page I will deliver the gift I promised on page one, and I will ask you to share your physical address so I can ship you a "box." The box would have a shock and awe, a gift of some sort, a book (preferably written by the marketer), and an invitation to take the next step (the brain-dead offer).

There is a school of thought that believes that you should only capture an email or name and email. They believe that asking for a telephone number in stage one will reduce your traffic to lead capture ratio. For what it's worth, I agree that asking for a telephone number and making it a required field will eliminate a few prospects who would have been okay giving you just their email. Personally, I am okay with not talking to prospects who are so concerned about their privacy that I cannot get their contact information.

My GOAL is to have a conversation with each prospect, identify their needs, and see if they qualify to be a client. Their privacy preferences are of little relevance to me. I just want to find out who I can talk to and whether or not they can buy! Once I am convinced that I want you as a customer, of course your preferences and priorities are of significant importance to me. (Please understand that this is an opinion, not an insight. I do not claim to have data to substantiate that my position is better. I just have a VERY FIRM opinion on this matter).

2. **Lead Conversion:** New Lead Follow-Up Sequence is included in this step. This is a three-to-five email

follow-up sequence with at least two telephone follow-up steps. The purpose of this sequence is to reiterate the message of the landing page and persuade the prospect to schedule an appointment with the marketer to discuss your mutual interests. If the prospect does not schedule an appointment, the prospect is placed on a LONG-TERM NURTURE sequence.

3. **Long-Term Nurture:** This is 24-month campaign that includes a quarterly print magazine, a monthly newsletter (no newsletter in the month you publish the magazine), a monthly holiday card in print, a twice-a-year gift of some sort, and a twice-a-year email newsletter. This is IN ADDITION to occasional special marketing efforts to convert an unconverted lead and lost opportunity.

4. **Appointment Confirmation Sequence:** When someone clicks to request an appointment, you want to send out information about the initial consultation, directions to your office (if it is an in-person appointment), rules of engagement, what you are trying to accomplish during the initial consultation, and what decision you expect them to make when they meet you for the first time.

5. **Appointment Prognosis Sequences:** There are only three prognoses of an initial sales appointment. There will be either an Appointment No Show, an Appointment No Sale, or Sold and Welcome to Our Practice. You want to have an email, print, and telephone sequence for each scenario, and the correct sequence should be triggered, depending on the prognosis of the appointment.

6. **Ascension and Tell-a-Friend Effort:** When the client makes the initial purchase, WHILE YOU ARE FULFILLING WHAT THEY BOUGHT, you want to ascend them into something else. If you don't sell them something else before the first transaction is over, you are dealing with a "lost customer reactivation situation," which is much more difficult compared to ascending an existing customer. Be prepared to have your next gig ready before you are even close to delivering the first product. Remember, a buyer is a buyer is a buyer is a buyer.

7. **Customer Long-Term Nurture:** This is important. Your customers should also get your long-term nurture. Your name should be in front of your prospects and your clients in a meaningful way.

This campaign will require development of about a dozen web pages, copy for about three dozen email messages, telephone scripts, and a substantial amount of print material. You may not be able to afford to spend that kind of money to nurture a prospect. That's okay. Go ahead and pretend that you CAN afford it, and get the print material developed as if you intend to ship the printed shock and awe to the prospect. If your revenue model does not justify printing a $20 shock and awe along with a $10 book in a $20 FedEx box, just send them a PRINTED LETTER inviting them to a URL where they can read your shock and awe online. Do NOT send an email asking them to click. They responded to your marketing effort,; now, respond to their response adequately.

You can use a software like Issuu.com to publish a digital publication and place it right on your website. Visit http://www.dentalgrowthmachine.com/ to read ALL the publications I have published on my website.

I never said it was going to be easy! It's not easy; it's not cheap; it's not quick. It takes blood, sweat, and tears to start a relationship, so when you get a client, don't let him go. Make a conscious effort to keep them.

IN/OUTSOURCING: YOU DON'T HAVE TO DO IT ALL

Even after standardizing, systemizing, and automating your sales lead generation, lead conversion, and sales processes, certain tasks will have to be done by humans.

The classic military analogy is "The Air force can soften the target, but the battle is won by the ground forces." Humans will have to close the deals.

There is a school of thought that believes in automation of sales processes. One of my close friends and JV partners works that way. Working with him is like working with an ATM. You go to his website, enter his funnel, watch his videos, and make an online payment; after that, you have to watch more videos and follow the instructions. The system works very well for him. He makes a lot of money, and he successfully trains the clients to follow those rules.

If that's how you want to live, you should talk to him. Call my office and ask me for an introduction to this fellow.

I am a lot more hands-on, touchy-feely guy. I spoil my clients with lots of attention from humans. Someone on my team is CONSTANTLY in touch with my clients. I share my mobile telephone number with my private clients, and my private email (pshah@eLaunchers.com) is checked on a half-dozen machines, and someone will respond to my emails within hours.

How much human interaction you wish to give to your clients depends on the nature of your business and your ability to invest in human resources to provide the interaction. The BIG DEAL is this: YOU do not have to do it all yourself. Even if you are a solo practitioner with NO staff, you can still hire a trained virtual assistant or train an intern to help you. (Read the intern productivity blueprint chapter in this book.)

There are many online resources that can facilitate hired help on an as-needed basis until you are ready to bring an in-house team. For years, we functioned with a formation of outsourced vendors until we grew to a point where we strategically started INSOURCING.

While there are resources like Upwork (formerly ODesk and Elance) Fiverr, and others, when we were outsourcing, we used Upwork extensively.

For the sake of cost effectiveness, you might want to consider looking at offshore labor in collaboration with onshore labor. We call it "rightshoring." There are a lot of excellent service providers with specific skillsets in the world that are referred to as "flat."

A word of caution as you outsource: You need to know how to buy, you need to know what to buy, and you need to be an excellent project manager. You also need to be a good QC expert, who can take delivery of various pieces of the puzzle from various vendors, QC each piece, put everything together and test end to end functionality of your system. This is not difficult; it is not rocket science–but it is time consuming.

I jokingly say, "I am so used to getting screwed, I got a budget for it." There is some truth to it. You not only need to develop tolerance for waste, negligence, and failure caused by human errors, but you also need to have a budget for it. I put away about 20 percent of my budget in a contingency allowance just to deal with these situations. The contingency fund is not always used on waste. Most of the contingency fund is used to deal with evolutions within projects, emerging threats, and evolving opportunities as the project progresses.

The key is to have adequate amount of cash on hand. Cash is your best friend. When you put enough money on the table, you have access to every resource you will need to deal with a situation. You can use cash to buy speed, buy accuracy, and buy enthusiasm. This might sound counter-intuitive, but you want to shift your focus from saving money to spending money. Spend as much money as necessary to get the work done when it is due.

As I said earlier in this book, going from zero to $100K is going to be different from going from $100K to $250K. Going from $250K to $500K is going to be a whole other journey altogether. When you take your business from $500K to about $100K per month, you will have the energy of a teenager. You will watch your business grow like a proud parent, but every stage of growth puts you in a different role. Your business is heavily dependent on you. Therefore, someone needs to take care of YOU.

So, find that perfect associate and train that person to be the wind under your wings. It will take some time for this person to get used to you, your habits, your way of working, your way of thinking, and your way of delegating. I always say, you need to give someone twelve weeks to fully ramp up.

The term you are looking for is "anticipation". You want your assistant to ANTICIPATE what your next move is and be prepared to finish execute it. Again, the anticipation comes after you establish your rhythm and share your values, promises, deliverables, processes, and protocols with your assistant in a consistent way. Once you and your assistant are on the same page with your rhythm, you are ready to standardize your sales lead generation and sales conversion theater. Once you standardize your sales lead generation and sales conversion process, you are now ready for systematization that will empower you to facilitate delegation and automation.

If you are considering hiring interns for your business, congratulations! You have made a BIG commitment to enrich someone's life, make a meaningful contribution to society, and develop your tomorrow's workforce.

I have been working with Montgomery College interns since 2009. Here's my story on how the whole internship program started and evolved in the words of the reporter who wrote this article:

ELAUNCHERS: COMBINING TECHNOLOGY & TRAINING TO GROW BUSINESSES

A NEW MARKETING FRONTIER

His company's techniques may be relatively new, but eLaunchers.com's founder Parthiv Shah isn't new to the direct marketing industry. He has more than 25 years of experience, beginning with direct mail in 1989 and incorporating data-driven, multi-channel direct marketing in 2002. Shah has always been on the cutting edge of the field; his company used a landing page with personalized URL technology as early as 2005 and conducted its first email marketing campaign in 2006. In addition, he has taught marketing at the University of Phoenix since 2002.

That industry-specific resume is only part of the reason eLaunchers.com has become a leader in direct marketing and communication automation. Shah also knows first-hand what it's like to start a small business and the consequences of failure. Though he's had many more successes than failures in his own nine (yes, nine!) entrepreneurial ventures, a dot.com company he launched in 1999 went bust. But he got right back to work, and by 2002 Shah had started a Boston-based premier mailing list company, which he sold three years later, making room for the debut of eLaunchers.com in 2006.

Unlike his previous entrepreneurial ventures, Shah didn't have to go it alone with eLaunchers.com. He found a modern-day "good Samaritan" in Dr. Hercules Pinkney, then Vice-President and Provost of Montgomery College Germantown Campus in Montgomery County, Maryland. New to the area, Shah needed someone who had critical local connections. "He shared with me his vision for his startup company—to become a locally grown— and nationally prominent data sciences and marketing automation company," Pinkney recalls. "He made a believer out of me."

Pinkney's faith was well placed. He facilitated some important introductions that helped build the foundation for eLaunchers.com, while Shah concentrated on creating the company he had pitched to his new friend. His approach was simple: Combine the best of his own marketing experience with the high-tech revolution that was separating successful businesses from unsuccessful ones. "eLaunchers.com automates the process of communicating with prospects, customers, and respondents," Shah explains. "The company is home to a crackerjack team of direct response marketing and technology professionals who share my passion for process automation."

That crackerjack team has assembled a suite of services that's truly remarkable. eLaunchers.com specializes in marketing technology, planning and strategy, creative services, web and app development, list and data services, and direct marketing services. So whether a client simply needs help with a website design—or requires an entire marketing campaign to be planned and implemented—eLaunchers.com is a one-stop resource.

The company is able to be all things to all clients because Shah's agile business adapts to changing technologies and improved methodologies. A passionate lifelong learner, he puts a priority on seeking out success strategies to benefit his clients. He points to Bill Glazer's book, *Outrageous Advertising That Is Outrageously Successful*, as being influential to his business model. Says Shah, "When I first saw him speak in 2009, what I took away was this: Do more for your clients than what they've paid for."

Bob Burg's *The Go Giver* also contributed to Shah's current approach, prompting the seasoned salesman to stop selling and start giving away his knowledge. "Some of the people who received my gifts came back and became clients," Shah reports. "That phenomenon doubled the size of my business from 2009 to 2010."

The third book that accelerated the growth of eLaunchers. com was *Conquer the Chaos* by Clate Mask, a guide to automating business processes using data as the core.

"Here's the bottom line: No one has time to do everything Dan Kennedy and Bill Glazer want you do to," Shah says of the marketing industry icons. "The key to success is automation— leveraging technology and business process automation to build a marketing and sales lead generation machine that produces awareness, converts awareness to qualified and responsive traffic on your website, converts traffic to conversation, and conversation into opportunities."

And it's all possible, he argues, without breaking the bank. With his "team of techies," the sky is the limit when it comes to return on a relatively small investment.

"I've made and lost a lot of money," Shah says. "With eLaunchers.com strategies, I'm able to share my experiences to help clients take advantage of what I've learned both from Bill Glazer, Dan Kennedy, and others, and from the University of Life."

Training the Next Generation of Marketing Experts

Shah, who was born in India and came to the U.S. in 1989, is an enthusiastic proponent of keeping American jobs in his adopted home country. He was also eager to thank Pinkney in a concrete way for all of his help in getting eLaunchers. com off the ground. In creating internship opportunities for Montgomery College students and other under-utilized populations—like veterans and stay-at-home moms—Shah was able to fulfill both goals.

The internship program, called Learn to Earn, is modeled after Mahatma Gandhi's "Buniyadi Talim" or Foundational Training. "Gandhi said that you can't declare physical independence without declaring fiscal independence first," Shah explains. "Gandhi taught Indian villagers to organize what they already know, identify what they don't have, find resources that can provide for their weaknesses, and build a whole deliverable that's market-worthy."

Indians used that model to declare fiscal independence from Britain—thanks to locally-made cloth that became more popular in India than what was being imported from England. "I'm using the same formula to make American students 'fiscally fit' so they can empower American employers to use American labor for the work currently outsourced to other countries," Shah says.

eLaunchers.com interns are treated to an educational experience beyond anything available in the classroom. The paid interns use study materials including books from marketing masters, Infusionsoft (an automation company) videos, Facebook management training videos from Seth Greene, mastermind series, and much more. In addition, they get one-on-one time with Shah and can access the company's dedicated Dan Kennedy reading room—the first of its kind in the world.

The internship experience is structured to incorporate both conceptual and concrete learning, as advocated by Pinkney, who joined eLaunchers.com in 2013 as Executive Leadership Advisor. Shah, the man who decided to give away his knowledge to potential clients, freely shares with interns his business formula, pricing, cost-volume profit analysis, and data science. "We teach them the art of how to use data to smell and chase money," he says. "I give them everything I've got, and they soak it up."

And unlike other internships, this one never ends. Even after students "complete" the program, they always have access to the mentor network and the training library, as well as the ability to fall back on eLaunchers.com resources if they're downsized or relocated.

It's clearly a concept that works. Of the 30 or so students, moms, and veterans who've gone through the internship, several have stayed on at eLaunchers.com as part of the core team, while the others are working at area businesses. Maybe that's because these employees come with a guarantee. eLaunchers.com vouches for their skills, attitude, aptitude, and work ethic, and even provides training or assistance once they've landed a job. Of his success in this area, Shah comments, "My trainees are potent, my trainees are honest, my trainees have basic business survival skills, and therefore, my trainees don't starve."

The program also has an employer component wherein eLaunchers.com teaches companies to "standardize, systematize, and automate" their workflow and processes so they can effectively use affordable American intern labor.

The Learn to Earn internships are a passion project for Shah rather than a big revenue source. But the work that he and Pinkney put into it is fueled by well-defined goals: "I want every American small business to employ at least one intern," Shah says. "I want Americans to buy American labor. I want American workers to be able to cost-effectively compete in the global marketplace. And I want to build an economic development task force."

He firmly believes that someday everyone will do business this way. His way. The eLaunchers.com way. Why is he so confident? Because his approach helps client companies grow their businesses exponentially while also allowing formerly under-trained interns—even immigrants who barely speak English—to achieve more than they ever thought possible. "I'm talking about me; I'm the first intern I trained," Shah shares. "I know how to make ends meet, no matter where the ends are."

He can help all business owners to do the same with their own companies.

HEY MOM, WHERE DO COMPANIES COME FROM?

Companies are born very much like human babies are born. The birth and life cycle of a child is very similar to the birth and life cycle of a business. People date; people mate; people conceive or come up with a business idea; they remain pregnant with the idea, and one day the business is born.

Sometimes, the baby cries in the middle of the night, and you have to wake up to take care of it. But a certain joy goes along with that parenting. Your baby business grows up, graduates, and makes its parents proud.

Parents sometimes have more than one child, in some cases twins. Many times in business, entrepreneurs have more than one opportunity to make money and bring in income. Like twins that require equal attention, care, and support, companies with more than one business venture require equal attention and maintenance. The same way babies require feeding, nourishment, and development, businesses require investment, cultivation, and support until they mature.

Like-minded children play together and learn the precious skills necessary to collaborate well with others. Similarly, it is helpful when entrepreneurs surround themselves with likeminded businesspeople. This type of collaboration and unity provides opportunities to birth new and innovative business ideas.

Act Now: If you are not already in a mastermind group, either start a group or join one.

Infant Mortality and Business Mortality

Most startup businesses fail and the mortality rate amongst new businesses is high. Many people lose their life's savings and end up in bankruptcy. Despite the statistics and the risks, small business ownership provides one of the best opportunities for success, independence, autonomy, creative freedom, and economic stability. If you can start and run a small business successfully, you will also be a good executive or employee in corporate America. It is the small businesses that survive the business infant mortality stage that are the foundation that keeps our economy stable and thriving. If you want to make a meaningful contribution to our economy and our nation, start a business and do not fail.

An entrepreneur's job is very unforgiving. As an entrepreneur you must be prepared to pay for every mistake, error, and fumble in judgment. At times, entrepreneurship requires a tremendous amount of belief and faith in yourself, and you must be your main cheerleader. Sometimes you find that you are your only cheerleader, but you must remain consistent and focus on bringing the business to maturity, just as a parent raises a child to adulthood.

Profits Drive Everything

Profits drive everything. If you are making profits, eventually everything else will catch up.

Many business owners focus only on the cash aspect of the business, but you need profitability to survive.

Profitability is what will sustain you through the infancy stage and the lead to your long-term survival.

Think of the Money First

Being an entrepreneur can be one of the most rewarding career opportunities. Along with the assumption of business risks, you reap the business rewards. Through distinguishing between good and bad opportunities and management of business risks, you can take control and implement successful business strategies, such as the formula for survival.

If You Want to be Somebody, BILL Somebody

It sounds funny, but it is true. If you can't bill anyone, you don't have a business!

Before you bill somebody, you must acquire permission to bill. What I mean by permission to bill is, you must prospect, pitch, close, collect, and deliver (hopefully in that order).

Possessing the ability to deliver a market worthy product is important, but just because you have the ability to deliver a market worthy product, it does not automatically mean that you will have permission to bill.

About Finding Work/Family Balance

If you have kids, remember the days (and nights) when your first born just came home from the hospital. You lost track of days, nights, weekends, home, work, family, and social life, and the little bundle of joy was the center of your universe. You slept as long as the baby allowed you to sleep. You ate when the baby allowed you to eat. You went to bathroom when the baby was taken care of. For the first 1,000 days of your company's life, be prepared to live like that. Don't expect anything from your company that you would not expect from your baby—in the first 1,000 days. Businesses are born and grow exactly like human babies. If you have a desire to find a work/family balance, go get a job.

Two Elements of Business

The two major elements of business are humans and money.

In the early days of starting a business, you will find yourself in an unbalanced economic state. You will find yourself living day-to-day, week-to-week, or month-to-month, and you will be frustrated that you are not able to accurately forecast your time and money budget. In difficult times like these, don't lose sight of how valuable your relationships are with people you are dealing with. It can take a lifetime to build trusting relationships with people, and a scuffle over a hundred bucks can ruin that.

Your frazzled state of mind and abnormal breathing patterns associated with a lack of financial security are not excuses for displaying distasteful behavior. The whole idea of "I would behave differently if I had the money" is unacceptable.

It is okay to love your money, but it is better to love your humans. Life is best when have great relationships with both, but if you must sacrifice one, sacrifice money. Remember, America has plenty of money and too few good humans. Take good care of American humans, and American money will take care of itself. I made a lot of money; I lost a lot of money. I made a lot of friends and did not lose any. Can you say that?

A friend once said, "The only thing bigger than Parthiv's head is Parthiv's heart." That's an interesting way to live. Sometimes I feel that people take advantage of me, but in general, I have been blessed with a measurable and impressive ROI for my "show of heart" way of business. I am building a company with a spiritual core that has a focus on pursuit of wealth. It is easier to pursue wealth if you have a balanced spiritual core and principle-centric leadership running your organization. This will help you find peace. And peace is absolutely necessary for prosperity.

SECRET FORMULA FOR SURVIVAL $COH > COB^T$

There is only one thing that stands between successful entrepreneurship and bankruptcy. This one thing is the formula for survival. Every business, even nonprofit organizations, must comply with this formula. You may already know what this timeless formula is. For some people, the one thing that equates to the formula for survival is common sense, but many of us lose sight of this valuable paradigm.

For the duration of time you are out of this formula, you are posting an irreversible capital loss. If you are borrowing money to fund your capital loss, eventually you will reach your maximum capacity to borrow, and the business will die. So, if you find yourself out of compliance with this formula, STOP BORROWING and focus on getting back in compliance with this formula.

Let's take a look at this formula that so many of us forget to focus on.

$(COH > COB)^t$

(Contribution to overhead must be greater than the cost of breathing)

$COH = REV\$ - (COS_\$ + COGS_\$)$

(Contribution to overhead) equals (revenue) minus (cost of acquiring the sale plus cost of goods or services sold)

REV$ = (Average Transaction $ x # of Transactions)t

(Revenue equals average transaction costs multiplied by the number of transactions, over time)

COB: The Cost of Breathing

The cost of doing business at zero revenue. Some people call it the cost of keeping the lights on or the cost of opening the door, etc. These are your actual out of pocket expenses for the period.

Glossary of Terms

COGS cost of goods (or services) sold

COS cost of acquiring the sale (commissions, marketing expenses, etc.)

COB out of pocket expenses at zero revenue

Revenue increases when the costs of transactions decrease (or remain low) and the numbers of transactions increase. To maintain or increase profitability, entrepreneurs will need to keep down the costs of acquiring sales (COS), costs of providing the goods or services sold (COGS), and the cost of breathing (COB).

$(COH \geq COB)^t$

The contribution of overhead always needs to be greater than the cost of breathing. This is a big point of contention with many people I talk to. When they are out of compliance, they call borrowing money an "investment."

"But you are losing money," I say, and they say, "If you look at it that way, my business will never succeed, so that is the wrong way to look at my business!" I think that is a problem.

Losing money is like getting on the wrong train. Time will do its damage if you remain on the wrong train. If you find yourself in an unfortunate situation where your deals are not profitable, you must get more money per deal or spend less money per deal. No, you cannot find an investor or a bank to fix this problem. You have to fix your deal.

I am not disrespecting the inherent business need to have access to infrastructure, overhead, capital, and resources. However, I am against picking a battle that you don't have a shot at winning. You may be on to something; you may have a great idea, but before you get pregnant with the concept, let us make sure that mother is healthy enough to carry the child.

Here is a piece of advice I got when I started my business in 2002. At the start of your business, don't focus on building your supply chain, business processes, and defining deliverables.

Just go out and prospect, pitch, and close. The first set of deals you bring in will define your processes and your deliverables, and they will help establish your supply chain. You will end up disappointing some folks, possibly lose money and look like a jackass in front of some very important people. That is a safer alternative than going into debt by making a heavy investment in infrastructure and resources, spending time negotiating with suppliers and work force, and developing scenarios as to who will do what when deals come. The advice I got was "just get the deals. Everything else will fall in place." This worked for me.

TECHNOLOGY BEHIND BUSINESS KAMASUTRA CAMPAIGN

Let's say that your social media has done its job. You have attracted your ideal prospect, patient, or client to your Facebook fan page. They liked your page. Then you ran clicks to website ads and drove this person off of Facebook to your website.

What happens once they get to your website?

If you are like 97% of most businesses, nothing happens.

You spent all that money on a website, why doesn't a click turn into business?

Does your website tell your prospect what you want them to do? Is that information displayed front and center, above the fold (on the screen without scrolling)? Is your website too cluttered?

After studying thousands of websites and working on hundreds of websites & landing pages, I developed a formula for building a "perfect" website. I call it Parthiv's Perfect Website Layout. There are others in the industry who might have a different opinion from me. If you don't think the layout I am describing in this chapter will be effective for you, please seek another opinion.

Here is my philosophy. There are four types of people visiting your website:

Clients who visit your website for logistical reasons (Login, request appointment, seek driving directions)

Prospects who have never heard from you before and are here for the first time.

HOT Prospects and referrals who are ready to interact with you and need a strong call to action.

Information seekers who want to read up on you, check you out, and build a trust and credibility in their own minds before they decide to engage.

In this layout we cater to ALL FOUR VISITOR SEGMENTS individually.

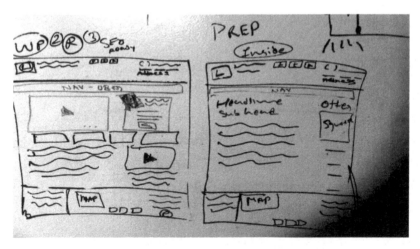

In Parthiv's perfect website layout, there should be a video or a slide show in the left 2/3rds area directly below navigation bar and a squeeze form to the right of video/slider. This area caters to prospects who have never been to your site before. The soft squeeze will get them started in a lead nurture sequence.

The squeeze form can be either a single offer squeeze, or it can have another layout:

- You can have multiple offer buttons in that area that would take you to an offer specific landing page.
- OR you can have one squeeze for with an option button for which free report you would like to read.
- Notice the four black boxes below the video and squeeze. These are called HARD calls to action. The four HARD Call to Action buttons cater to warm and to hot prospects and referrals that come to your website who know you, who have seen your stuff before, and who are ready to make an initial commitment. We always recommend following four HARD OFFERS.
- Special Offers
- Current Events
- Testimonials
- Tell-A-Friend

The interior pages are offer/product-specific squeeze pages with HARD calls to action, like "Buy Now" or "Download a Coupon/Gift Certificate."

The header area will be constant all through the website. The header area will also be visible on the mobile friendly responsive layout. Therefore, the header should not be a ONE BIG IMAGE. It should be a collage of multiple elements including:

- Your logo
- Your tag line
- Your telephone number (as text, not as image)
- Your social media buttons
- Your customer friendly interaction buttons like:
- Login to portal
- Request Appointment
- Driving Directions

Now let us look at this layout in action. Here are a couple of pictures:

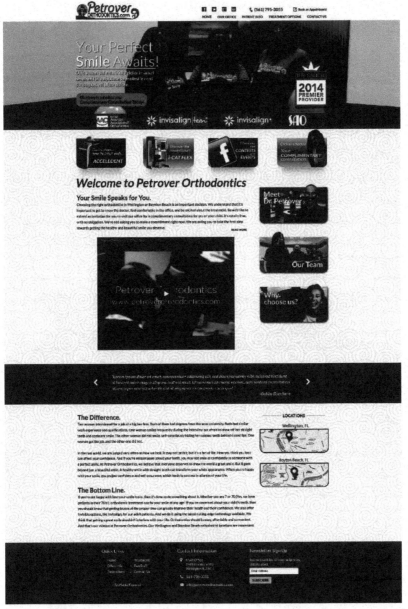

These sites are clean, comforting, and professional. On the right – where your eyes go first is a Squeeze form where you are offering a free report or a free 3-video course when they fill out your form. Now the prospect has entered your funnel, and you can start your communications with them.

Under that offer is their monthly newsletter and monthly video update.

In short, it is an easy to understand website with multiple clear calls to action that result in very sophisticated follow up marketing.

What would make it even better is if the lead generation campaign that led the prospective patient to a specific landing page on the site that only referenced the offer that was made on the campaign. That way the visitor would know they were on the right page and will not mistakenly sign up for anything else before doing what they came there to do.

If this whole process of attraction, engagement, and conversion seems familiar to you, it should. It's just like sex.

Think about it: you will find the concept of understanding relationships between businesses and their customers very much like understanding how relationships are built between two humans. Let's talk about sex. How does it work? Well, the first step is segmentation. You don't want to sleep with just anybody; you want to be picky about who you choose.

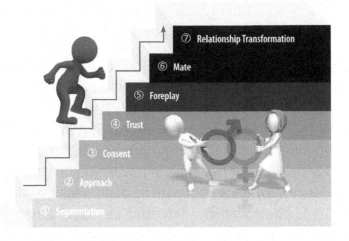

Once you know who you are, once you know who you want to go after, then you are going to organize, orchestrate and execute an approach.

Do you walk up to the first man or woman you meet in a bar and ask them to marry you? Of course not, the woman would throw a drink in your face (or otherwise reject you) 99 times out of 100. You want to approach them in the right way. You are seeking **consent.** And you are not going to get consent for mating; you are hopefully going to get consent for dating, so your **message** should focus on dating.

Once you approach someone, what happens? Will they ignore you? Will they like you and give you consent to continue the conversation, or they will get upset that you had an audacity to approach them?

If you are not meant to be together, accept the "No thank you" and move on. The world is filled with other opportunities. There are plenty of fish in the sea.

Let us say you are successful in persuading someone to raise their hand and say, yes they are interested in talking to you (or getting your irresistible free offer). Now what do you do? They didn't give you consent to mate; they only gave you consent to date. So date.

What happens during the dating and courtship period? How long should you date? While you are dating, what are you going to do? You are going to establish trust. How do you establish trust? Trust is a very mathematical thing. In my opinion, trust is 10% emotions and 90% mathematics. You can build your business in a way, so you can establish trust with whomever you wish to build a relationship with. If trust is controlled by data and can be mathematically measured, you can manage and maintain trust. You can elevate trust. You can improve your intimacy by increasing levels of trust.

How do we do this from a marketing perspective? First, you have to deliver what you promised.

If you offered a free report as your lead generation magnet on social media, there should be:

An instant PDF download of that report,

An opportunity to receive a hard copy via direct mail (to capture their full contact information),

Perhaps an email that goes out right away with a link to download the report, and maybe, just maybe

A tell-a-friend page where the prospective customer can send their friends a copy of the report as well.

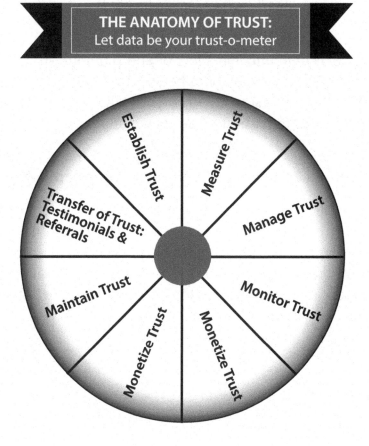

THE ANATOMY OF TRUST:
Let data be your trust-o-meter

We are going to talk about monetization of trust. That's the mating part. Hopefully, dating and courtship will reach a point where you get consent for intimacy. You are approaching a point where you are about to get consent to get intimate. When you do get consent for intimacy? It is a very delicate moment.

What does mating mean from a business standpoint? You are about to make your first sale.

Now that you see where this is all going, let's break it down into bite-sized manageable chunks.

What is your irresistible free offer? Do you have one? Does it convert well? What I mean by conversion is, if 100 people were to visit that offer, how many of them would take you up on it? How do you know if you should be happy with the number of people who take you up on that offer? Every industry is different, and every offer is different. We would be happy to give you some perspective as to how many people should be signing up for your offer- if you call us at 301.760.3953 to request a free consultation.

You see? I just practiced what I preach. I made another offer to you if you are ready to take the next step with us.

In order to craft an irresistible free offer that gets a good number of ideal prospects to sign up for it, you have to think like a prospect. What do they want? What pain are they in that is leading them to seek you out? What keeps them up at night? What are they hoping someone like you can do for them?

In the case of http://www.eLaunchers.com, our clients are small business owners with $500K to $2.5MM (and $2.5M to $10M) in revenues, and they fiercely compete against larger rivals with deeper pockets. They often feel like they need 18 arms to run their businesses. They don't have enough hours in the day to get done everything they need to, let alone learn all they want about marketing their business. They are tired of money going out the back door of their company without enough coming in the front door at a much faster pace. They are frustrated with how demanding their business has become. Sometimes they feel like all they did was create a job for themselves that doesn't pay enough for the level of stress they have to deal with. They lay awake at night wondering when it will ever get easier.

Does that sound like you? If so, then you will love our "Step-by-Step Profit Multiplying Marketing Automation Blueprint. " You can visit www.eLaunchers.com (home page) and click on "Your Success Blueprint" to request this publication.

When you communicate your irresistible free offer to your target market, you are looking for one of the following reactions:

1. How do you do that?

2. How can I get one of those?

3. Where have you been all my life?

If you get one of those reactions or they offer to give you money on the spot to alleviate their pain, then you know you hit the nail on the head.

You want them thinking that you understand them and make them wonder if you have installed a secret web cam in their office (that's a joke – forgive my Indian sense of humor).

So let's review what we have done so far.

Picked a target market that has a pain that you can get rid of and that can afford to pay you what you want to charge to fix this pain.

Crafted an Irresistible Free Offer that follows Dan Kennedy's proven copywriting formula. For more on this formula you should get a copy of *The Ultimate Sales Letter* book by Dan Kennedy and the Magnetic Marketing course by Dan Kennedy. The formula is: Problem – Agitate – Solve. You want to identify their problem, make sure they are agitated by it, and then position the next step with you as the solution for their pain.

Ideally you would use Infusionsoft to capture their contact information, deliver the irresistible free offer, and follow-up with them to take the next step with you.

Of course you need to promote that offer to your target market.

Next, let's hypothesize that all this has worked. Your ideal client, prospect or patient, clicked on the ad to like your Facebook fan page. Then they clicked on the ad from your fan page that took them to your website. There they signed up for your offer, and you delivered it to them. Congratulations! You have just established trust. You did what you said you were going to do. Now you need to get them to take the next step in your relationship.

- That next step could be:
- Opening your next email
- Clicking on a link in the next email you send them
- Sharing your Facebook fan page on their news feed so that their friends see it
- Filling out a Tell a Friend form on your website to spread the word about you
- Using your website to book a consultation with you
- Attending an event (either in-person or online)
- Coming to your office
- Buying something from your website
- Showing up at your store or restaurant with some type of tracking code that lets you know how they got there

You get the idea. This list is only limited by your imagination.

No matter what you have them do, you need to make sure you can track that behavior. As you can imagine, the more ways they have to interact with you, the more data that behavior will generate inside of their contact record in your customer relationship management or marketing automation software.

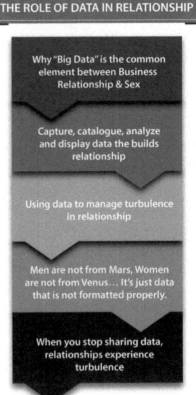

Let's talk about how you manage and monetize all of that data, or as I like to call it – establishing your rhythm.

Why is establishing rhythm important? Because without rhythm you will be randomly doing things that may or may not help you get to where you want to go with regard to your new relationship with your new prospect.

For establishing the rhythm, we create an annual marketing calendar. It has a list of proposed daily marketing activities, weekly marketing activities, monthly marketing activities, quarterly marketing activities, and annual marketing activities. The calendar also has a marketing ROI calculator and a monthly marketing expense budget.

So, how do you go about establishing your rhythm and why don't you feel that you have a rhythm already established? Do you feel that you have a bunch of people living and working on an island, and they just do whatever they do, but there is no synchronization or harmony among them?

Fortunately, you are not alone. Most growing businesses have this problem. Some often refer to it as "growing pains," but in reality, this is a problem that can be avoided or fixed.

Take the time to build up your central database. Once the central database is built, connect your current apparatus and your current humans to the new rhythm and train them.

If your business is at $500,000 to $2,000,000 in revenues, you might benefit from a workflow called Magnetic Marketing Implementation A.B.C.D. from eLaunchers.com. To request a copy of this publication, please visit <u>www.eLaunchers.com/start</u> or call my office at 301.760.3953. Be sure to ask for the digital, fillable PDF of the book. This booklet has the same workflow at a much higher sophistication. Using Infusionsoft Perfect Customer Lifecycle, I built a campaign in Infusionsoft called Business Kamasutra Benchmark campaign. Here you will see that you are spending money on marketing to drive traffic to a landing page or home page; you would capture the lead, deliver a free report, add them to <u>new lead sequence,</u> and persuade them to request an appointment. They are also automatically added to your long term nurture sequence. The prospect is placed on the telephone list to call and followup. Your staff member will make the call and fill out the call prognosis form. Based on the call prognosis the prospect will be added to '<u>connected – appointment made, connected – no appointment, connected – follow up, connected –don't call back, and left voicemail</u>'

sequences. Each sequence will loop the prospect back to the call list until the appointment is requested. When they request an appointment you would add them to the pre appointment sequence and send them your welcome kit or shock and awe. On the day of appointment you would fill out the appointment outcome form, so the prospect is placed in the appropriate sequence: appointment no show, appointment no sale, or welcome to our practice. Once the client is part of the family they are added to the NPS (Net Promotor Survey) sequence.

In this survey we ask ONE question. On a scale of 1 to 10, how likely are you to introduce us to a friend or colleague. If the score is 7 or higher, you are added to the promotor sequence, so we can send you referral marketing material. This is ONE end to end Infusionsoft campaign that captures the spirit of Business Kamasutra workflow and implements it in your business.

The picture in this book is going to be too small to read. This is just a visual of what the campaign actually looks like. It is a bit complex, but it provides complete, end to end functionality to your perfect customer lifecycle. If you visit www.businesskamasutra.com and fill out the form, I will send you a companion booklet called Business Kamasutra passport that has larger, color image.

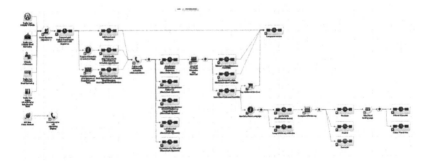

I just made you another irresistible free offer. Do you remember how many of them I have made in this one small chapter?

I offered you my book: *Business Kamasutra*

I offered you my Business Kamasutra Benchmark Campaign Blueprint,

I offered you the Step-by-Step Profit Multiplying Marketing Automation Blueprint

I offered you the Magnetic Marketing Implementation A.B.C.D. (Any Business Can Do).

I offered you a free consultation by calling us at 301.760.3953 to request a free consultation, or you can go to www.eLaunchers.com if you are ready to take the next step to learn more about how your business can harness the power of automation and big data to help generate even bigger profits with less stress.

I look forward to hearing from you!

Parthiv Shah, CEO
www.eLaunchers.com

RESOURCES

TECHNOLOGIES

This is a partial list of technologies I use and recommend. For a complete list of technologies we recommend, please visit our website at www.eLaunchers.com/client and book an appointment with me. Remember, the technologies I am recommending are MY PREFERENCES at the time of making these recommendations. Please take this recommendation list as my opinion. If you are using alternative technologies, that is not necessarily a bad thing. I have my favorites, and I have my reasons for it. If you do become my private client and we actually work for you, we will be using the technologies of my choice because that is what we know how to support, and that is what my team is trained on.

- ☐ Marketing Automation: Infusionsoft, Hubspot, Active Campaign.
- ☐ Graphic design: Adobe InDesign, Illustrator, Photoshop, Apple Pages, Microsoft Publisher
- ☐ Web Hosting: www.wpengine.com
- ☐ Web site design: Wordpress.com or Hubspot CMS.
- ☐ Landing pages: Hubspot, Optimize Press (WP), Leadpages.net, Instapage.com, Clickfunnels.com
- ☐ Membership sites: CustomerHub, Imember360, WordPress Wishlist, Memberium.
- ☐ Social media integration with Infusionsoft: Hubspot
- ☐ Application integration with Infusionsoft: Zapier
- ☐ PCI Compliance and ecommerce credit card processing: Authorize.net and QuickBooks Online
- ☐ Video editing: Adobe Premier, Video Scribe
- ☐ Cloud Computing: Microsoft Office 365

- ☐ Online Calendar and Appointment Scheduling: Hubspot
- ☐ Note-taking: Microsoft OneNote
- ☐ Mobile Technology for the Road: Samsung Note 10 (for 2019), Microsoft Surface Pro (For 2019)
- ☐ Cloud file storage: Dropbox, Box, Microsoft OneDrive
- ☐ Project Management and Team collaboration: www.Monday.com or Basecamp.
- ☐ Email marketing (small budget or free tools): Hubspot Free or Starter Growth stack.
- ☐ Video recording and editing training: www.tabletvideotraining.com
- ☐ Copywriting: Montblanc and Cartier :-)
- ☐ Text messaging: www.fixyourfunnel.com
- ☐ Call capture and reverse data append: www.fixyourfunnel.com
- ☐ List research: www.srds.com and www.acculeads.com
- ☐ Data intelligence and data cleansing: Windowbook.com tools, Oracle for database programming.
- ☐ Online data storage: MySQL
- ☐ Preferred programming language: PhP
- ☐ Online meeting: www.gotomeeting.com
- ☐ Reporting and analysis tools: Hubspot, Databox, Google.

FREQUENTLY ASKED QUESTIONS FOR PARTHIV SHAH

Q. How did eLaunchers get started?

A. I have been in the Direct Marketing space since 1989. Within the Direct Marketing space, I have been in Database Marketing, List Marketing and Data intelligence from 1989 until 2002.

I left my job working for a direct mail company to start my own Direct List Business in 2002, List Launchers. I sold List Launchers in 2005, and I took some time off; then, I started eLaunchers.com.

It evolved into a turnkey marketing communication firm that essentially offers a data-centric transaction focused automatic marketing integrating email, online marketing, offline marketing, and telephone marketing.

All of it leads up to driving prospects into a squeeze page on the homepage, a campaign-specific URL, or a personalized URL.

It persuades a prospect to leave their name, email, and phone number, captures that information, and builds a sales funnel that leads up to an initial appointment; or if we cannot get an initial appointment, we will put them into a long-term nurture. That's what we do.

Q. Who is your ideal client?

A. My ideal client is a professional practice that makes money by appointment. So, a dentist or an orthodontist, a physician, an attorney, a financial advisor, or an info marketer.

Now within that industry, I want people with the right mindset, who understand the value of an automated lead generation, lead capture, and lead conversion theater. In general I have very little tolerance for price sensitivity or skepticism. If I have to justify my existence in your life, I already lost; we should just part ways. I am not a pitch/ propose or compete kind of a guy.

I also do very well with companies that are spending money on marketing but are unhappy with the results that they are generating.

The process that we build puts measuring devices on your current marketing materials to help you determine what's working and what's not working. That way you can actually go in and figure out what you should do to turn on the heat, what you should tone down, or what you should turn off.

Q. Who are you?

A. I am a data scientist. I am a direct marketer. If I have to describe my talents in one phrase, I smell and chase money, and I use data to do it.

Everything else revolves around that. I basically have three skills.

I can spot an opportunity, and that comes to me from my military background. I can scan the landscape and know what is an opportunity and what is a trap. Life is like a video game to me.

When I walk into a foreign territory, I am looking for food and for clients. I am looking for strengths and looking for what can hurt me; then, I am on my own path.

When I was in an MBA class, I had the privilege of working with professors from Harvard. There I learned the eight-paradigm SWOT analysis method.

Dr. Michael Porter's SWOT analysis method is based on the theory of competitive relativity. If you Google "theory of competitive relativity" and "Dr. Michael Porter," it is explained in layman's terms.

I measure/catalog your SWOT analysis, and once we build these four quadrants, we then build four additional quadrants. This is the anatomy of a grand slam home run. When you hit a home run, you will know right after the bat connects with the ball. It's a perfect pitch, your shoulders are in the right place, and the bat is in the right place.

That's what I do.

I look for battles to pick, where winning the battles will be significant and losing won't be embarrassing. That's my plan number one.

Plan number two, I have the capacity to paint your picture with myself in it. I can use the same skill to paint your prospect's picture with you in it.

And the third thing, I know exactly how to ask for an order, without alienating the relationship. Not only do I know that, but my data matrix tells me when to ask for an order. It's all about trust. It's all about establishing, monitoring, measuring, and monetizing trust in real time. Data can be your guide, and that is who I am.

Q. Why is Dr. Burleson telling me that you should do this?

A. Because I am a data scientist, and you will not do this. Dr. Burleson gets you pregnant, and I will help you deliver the baby.

Dr. Burleson is an interesting dentist. He is better at Infusionsoft than I am. He is better at WordPress than two thirds of my staff.

He is better at Photoshop and Adobe illustrator than all of my graphic designers combined. He is better at copywriting than 99 percent of humans on this earth, and he is also a damn good dentist and a good philanthropist.

You are trying to build your business as does Dr. Burleson, you are not him. You do not have time to do everything that needs to be done to build that Burleson spirit in your business. You don't have the skills that Burleson has. You have never logged into Adobe Illustrator and Photoshop. You are going to need a half-dozen different software programs and hundreds of hours on top of your already busy schedule.

If you don't hire me or someone like me, you are going to hire someone in your office or you are going to promote someone in your company, and it is going to be a very painful process.

Now working with me can be frustrating and painful, but at least I have a process to relieve your frustration and manage your pain.

It will be hard for you to learn a system, learn a protocol, and implement it in your life. That's why Dr. Burleson recommends me. Somebody has to do the work. How about hiring a guy who is the Indian behind Burleson to do your work?

Q. How much does it cost?

A. A lot. And it's a significant relationship.

It takes more than money to do this. I won't just be needing money, but I am also going to need you. I am going to need your time. I am going to need your attention, and this won't be done overnight.

This is not a machine; this is not a product, and I don't have a coaching program. I am doing all the work.

So, here is how the relationship starts. First thing we need to do is meet. I need you to come to Germantown, MD. We spend about a day and one-half together. We will meet in the afternoon. I will ask you a whole bunch of questions.

I will understand….
- who you are,
- why you are,
- what you are,
- where you are,
- where should you be going,
- what can we do together to help you win,
- what's the probability of winning.

I need a total of 14 hours of in-person time just for whiteboarding, talking, and making decisions at a very detailed, tactical level. This is a retreat for your business, and it will make you tired. I had a situation when a couple arrived at the airport, and we went to my house for dinner. At 9:30pm, I just drove them to office to pick up my laptop, and I heard the lady scream, "Oh no, we are at the office again".

I don't get tired. I work very hard. It could be a very long day and a half. It is fun for the most part. And the next day, we begin drawing. We build a mindmap of what can be done for your business.

We do the SWOT analysis and draw it out; we then build a marketing automation plan, and we build an Infusionsoft perfect customer life cycle.

We draw out what assets you already have in place that will yield to this marketing makeover, and we will put together the taskforce, the task list, task timeline, and budget.

The fee for the initial consultation is $7500 (more if I travel to you). At the end of the consult, if you think that it wasn't worth your money and time, I will not only return your money, but I will drive you to the airport myself.

If you decide to go forward, the fee for the full marketing makeover is $25K–$85K all-but-copy. We do what it takes to get you money. I have a list of 486 tasks that we may perform for you. We will give you the list and say that these are the tasks that we intend to do for you, and we will do whatever you and I feel is necessary. We may or may not do certain things. We might end up adding more things. You might not need one website; you might need three. You will also have a comprehensive list of the things that I don't do. And for things that I can't do, I will tell you who to contact to get them done.

We do whatever it takes to make you win. My initial consultation comes with a 100 percent money-back guarantee. We do not guarantee success. I don't always achieve success. In fact, you can expect that half the things

I do will not generate a positive return on the money you invest.

I am not guaranteeing success. I don't have a silver bullet. I do guarantee that you will be happy.

If at the end of the consultation day, we feel that this is not right for you, I will invite you to ask me for a refund. I am perfectly willing to write off my losses and move on rather than lose a friend, because another practitioner in your zip code will want to buy what we created for you. If I didn't do a good job, I would rather lose money than lose faith.

In addition to the marketing makeover, I also have a managed marketing services that serves as HMO for your entire marketing department. My tech team, my Marketing automation team, my data team, my print production team, my web team, my project management team, my people in India, my people in California, my people in Germantown, and my interns all work for you.

What is the reason for our multithousand dollar monthly fee? If I am unable to do what it takes to make you win, we will gently break away from each other. There's no pain of disconnecting to you, only I will have that.

Everything I do is in your ecosystem. For example–your website is hosted on my server, until you want to host it somewhere else. It's in your Infusionsoft, connected to your practice management system. It's your API bridge that you are buying directly from DENTMA. You can terminate our relationship without having anything else to break.

You tell me to leave, I begin packing, and as long as another competent person is doing what I used to do, I will not take a mission critical piece of your life and leave.

Q. How long does it take?

A. It can take between six weeks and six months, depending mostly on you. We aim for 100 days to finish.

Q. What do I have to do?

A. You will need to write, or you will work with a writer I recommend. We have writers trained for our program. We only work with writers that are in our system. You will need to approve the content. You will be approving the strategy.

The most important thing is that this is your business, and I need to capture your spirit and show it to the world as intended by you. I am creating your avatar in paper, pixel, and plastic. I can't do that without you. So when I need you, I need you. I will be asking for your private email that goes to your cellphone.

I will ask for your cellphone number, and when I need you I will ask for an appointment. We also expect that you read what we give you, and you give us feedback on time. If you don't, we will nudge you. If you don't respond to a nudge, we will nudge you aggressively. If you don't respond to our aggressive nudge, we will wait for you, and we will wait for your attention.

Now, we also expect you to be happy. This is not a black box. This is built to your taste, to your satisfaction. So, if you don't like something, we expect you to tell us, so we can fix it. You are not wasting our time. If I need to scrap something and start it over, I am going to do that. You don't have to be reasonable, you have to be happy.

If you are unhappy, you will leave. But I want you in my life for years to come. So you have to make a conscious and timely effort to play your role and tell me what it takes to make you happy. That's my deliverable. If you are writing your own copy or if you are going to do something in WordPress or Infusionsoft, we expect that you report that to our project manager. When I say you, it means your entire ecosystem (you may have other ad agencies, you may have staff members, you may have other vendors, etc.).

We need to include the mass one cohesive force, one united front towards the common goal. But when you buy my system, by default you are putting me as an admin of your entire theater. My staff, you, your staff, your vendors, and their staff, will report to my project manager, my production manager, and my timeline. That's what you have to do.

Q. Why should I go through this?

A. Well, at the end of the day, my process does four things: get clients, keep clients, sell treatments, and get referrals. If I don't do it, somebody else will have to do it, or it will not get done. The core purpose of implementing a marketing automation system is reducing dependency on humans and putting a system in place, which does its job day in and day out. Have you watched Spongebob Squarepants? He makes Krabby Patties. There is no system to it. There are no standards to it. There's no process to it. That's why Mr. Krabs only has one location.

You want to do this because you are the owner– you are the ringleader of the whole circus. Try taking a step back from it and seeing if your world can function without you. How are you going to retire? If you are working hard and are unhappy with your income and cannot work any harder, how are you going to grow? How are you going to do more than one location? What if you want to sell your business? Who's the buyer who wants to buy your business? Can they walk into a systematized lean mean marketing machine that is generating a steady flow of leads?

Lead generation is not as critical as lead conversion. Any ad agency, any decent marketing communications company will have a capacity to generate the leads at the top of your funnel.

If you do not have an adequate conversion theater, if you do not have your people, paper, pixel, and plastic tastefully organized, you will always be dependent on the skills of your people. I can program paper, I can program plastic, and I can program pixels. I cannot program people. People need to do what I tell them to do. If you had a choice, who would you rather depend on, paper, pixel, and plastic, or people? Your call.

Q. How does it work?

A. Well, it's simple: You pay, I work, you watch.

Once you pay, it's my responsibility to take you or drag you to the finish line. We work together, after we are engaged for the marketing. Let me answer the question in three parts:

How does the consultation work?

We schedule a day, you get on a plane, you come over. Before that, you want to FedEx me any or all marketing materials that you have. Send me a list of your URLs that you own. Get me a list of all your people who are involved in your marketing lead generation, lead conversion, and any other humans that I should know about, and what role they play. I don't want to step on anybody's toes.

Basically, usher me into your world before we meet. If you have done direct mail marketing before, you probably would have received some returned mail that was undeliverable. Send that mail to me. If you have very large pieces of mail, just peel off the yellow sticker that the post office puts on. I want to read your sticker. When I look at your returned direct mail, it gives me a certain amount of information about the health of your data, your list, and stuff like that. It prepares me for our conversation when you come.

I need a total of fourteen hours. You will be here for a one or two-night stay! If there's anything else that you want to work on while you are here, bring it with you. I don't do anything else except take care of you when you are on the floor. We call it client-on- the-floor. When we have client-on-the-floor, I will have my complete attention towards you. Anything that you want goes into my mind map. At the end of our discussion, I print those big mind maps and give you copies to put on your wall and check things off as we get them done for you.

How does the process work for a marketing makeover?

I have a team of direct marketers, data scientists, graphic designers, computer programmers, and Infusionsoft programmers.

The only people who we don't have on staff are the people who write copy. I am the best English speaking man that my company has. I don't write. This book that you are reading. I didn't write it. Somebody talked to me and helped me come up with what to put in this publication.

As long as you are willing to write the English part, we have you covered for everything else. We have swipe files and example content/copy ready for you. For custom copy, we have a team of writers you can hire. (You pay the writers directly.)

There are five elements of marketing at a DNA level: arts, linguistics, time, money, and data. I am an expert at time, money and data. I have in-house resources to do art that whacks me up on time, money, and data.

Once we are engaged, we need what I call a preparation period of about four to nine days. That's how much time I need to huddle with my team and dissect what I promised you. You will start hearing from my team members, who will basically be looking at their roles and what they need to do.

They will begin by asking you for your digital assets like logos, entry into your web world, your Infusionsoft, your data, etc. Then we start taking things into our custody. Our project manager will dissect the mind map and create a project plan (who is assigned what task, when it needs to be done by, etc.).

You will get your set of workload assigned to you. If you didn't hire a copywriter, you will be assigned the writing work. We are going to tell you what we need you to write. We might say we need eight emails for this, we need an email for the thank you page on your website, we need a refer-a-friend letter written, etc. At any point if you are struggling, I have professional resources that are willing to help, and they are a phone call away. All we have to do is schedule them.

We have resources that will hold your hand through the content creation if you need that help.

If you hire one of our writers, we work integrate the writer in the project.

All through that process, you will schedule a call about once a week with my project manager, who will give you a status report and ask you for your share of work. If you are behind or if there is something that you want that was not discussed previously, you will go ahead and make that wish to the project manager, and he/she will assign the work to someone else.

I report to the project manager, just like you will report my share of work. Here's some of what will be on my plate: all the list research, data science work, acquisition of data, utility control, looking at incoming data, sending the data for cleansing, modeling, etc.

I do all that work myself, and I usually have a junior data scientist watching me to make sure that I am doing what I intend to do. We follow the pilot-copilot model, so whenever I work, somebody always quality controls my work. If somebody else is working, I will quality control their work. All work is always watched by four eyes in real time as the work is done. We have real time quality control on data work. For everything else, web, data, technology, etc., we have a quality control team that does our internal quality control work.

I have teamed up with three to four other Infusionsoft ICCs and Hubspot developers, who basically check my work before delivering it to you. By the time anything comes to you, it has been looked at by about a half–dozen different people. So, it is highly unlikely that you will find something that is factually wrong or not as intended.

I can't say that about copy. Because it is a different set of quality control guidance, rules are followed, and you will play a very critical role in approving proofs before we go live or before we print something. You may request services of a proof reader/ editor.

You will have a monthly call with me or one of my team members (if you are on our monthly maintenance program). We look at our progress from the previous month.

If you have something that we should implement or if I have an idea that I should offer to you, then we will discuss that. If I am doing something for you that has spectacular results, I will show it off to the rest of my tribe. Vice-versa, if I have done something for someone, I will show you how it has worked. I will introduce to you, so that you can talk to my other clients, and you can brainstorm together. A lot has come out of my clients' talks with each other and strategizing as a tribe. I can tell you, "I have four other orthodontists who are doing this exact campaign. Would you like to talk with them?" Everyone in the eLaunchers world is wired to share their opinions. I expect the same from you. You will help your fellow eLaunchers clients and share your opinions, your successes, your horror stories, etc.

Again, it's a very open and transparent environment. When we do a campaign of the month, you have access to our web, data technology, and graphic teams. We do whatever needs to be done, month in and month out, for your marketing and marketing automation.

Sometimes, we do a lot in a month; sometimes, we don't do much; some months are more profitable than others, and that's how it is done.

Q. How do I get ROI on my investment?

A. Well, you may or may not get ROI on your investment. Your money is truly at risk. The first thing I ask people is how bad it will it hurt if they have to write off the investment that they are making.

I do not have a silver bullet; I do not have a magic pill. I can't wave a magic wand. We will take steps to mitigate risks; we will use common sense as our guide, but your money is truly at risk. I am on the edge of my seat until we reach the first fiscal milestone. I want our relationship to be a zero-sum game.

My first goal is to sell at least one treatment, so you are getting money in your hands out of our joint efforts. I am looking for that much money in the vicinity using a common sense test before I encourage someone to buy. If I am not comfortable, I will tell you that I am worried— that it is not going to work. I cannot predict success, but I can predict failure with precision accuracy. If I tell you something is going to fail, take my word for it– it will not work. So call it a blessing; call it a curse, but I have a capacity to tell you something is not going to work out.

The second milestone I have is a three-times return. If you are investing $3,000 with me, you need to generate $9,000 in revenue because you are going to have overhead costs, and you are going to have the cost of goods sold, and you are going to have an expectation of profit. So, you are determining whether or not you want to continue working with me, whether or not you want to fire me, or whether you are happy or not.

You need to keep two things in mind. At what point do you get all your money back? What is generating three times the cost of it, and what is generating under three times? Anything generating over three times is a jackpot. We standardize it; we systemize it, and we keep doing that and we tell the rest of the tribe. For anything that is doing less than three times, we keep tweaking it until we reach that magic three times goal.

Now remember, I am not promising you three times, and I am not promising you a positive ROI. I am not promising you that you will make a dime out of the money that you are investing in me. I am just telling that you will be happy with our relationship. If you are not, I will invite you to ask me for your money back, and if you do so, somebody in your immediate vicinity probably will pick up the scraps of the pieces that I have built. That's what I have to say on ROI.

Q. Who else have you done this for, and what were their results?

A. For dentists/orthodontists: I have had the privilege of doing data intelligence and dental marketing work for some of the top of the class in the Dan Kennedy world. I was invited to play with Dr. Tom Orent's system, and with the mastermind members of Dr. Charlie Martin. People who attended an event hosted by Jerry Jones or hosted by Whitehall have used our services. Of course private clients of Dr. Dustin Burleson use us, and the people who attend his events and buy his info products. I have also worked for physicians, other clinicians, attorneys, financial advisors and information marketers in Kennedy circle.

I have had the privilege of not just learning from these guys but also working for them; they all have good things to say about me. I am proud to have a growing list of references who not only will cheerfully record a video for me, but routinely attend events where I am exhibiting, and spend two to three hours at my booth and tell people how they feel about working with me.

Do I win all the time? No. With every day that goes by, I am evolving, I am getting better. We are getting better; we are becoming a better company. If we aren't meant to be together, I will engineer my exit from you, in such a way that only I get hurt. I can always make money, if not from you then from somebody else.

You can go to eLaunchers.com/testimonials, watch some videos, and read some testimonials. Or their names are there with their picture. Pick up a phone and call them. As a matter of fact, if you become my client, someday I will ask you to be on this list. I will want you to talk to my prospects; I will want you to attend some events, come to my booth, and encourage others to become clients. I cannot grow my business without endorsements.

So when you hire me, I ask you, "What are your win conditions?" What do I have to do to get you to introduce me to your friends and people that you can influence?

About 90 percent of my business comes from referrals, from my referral partners and existing clients, and events that I attend or exhibit at. I practice what I preach; I use the same tools that I am recommending to you; I use the same team that I am recommending to you. It's an open game, and if something does not work, I don't hide anything under the rug. We dissect the problem, learn from the mistake, and we move on or redeploy.

Q. Once this is implemented, what work does my staff have to do?

A. We will discuss that in great detail at the initial consultation. That depends on your staff; that depends on their technical aptitude, and that also depends on how much work is deliberately assigned to your humans by the system.

Most businesses work like this: They start with a human, give the human some apparatus, put together a workflow in the system, and as the business grows, they add more humans. Then those humans bring their own appliances and apparatuses, and the data flows where it may.

In my system, we start from the end. We build a data system; we defer the apparatus to the data system, and we defer the humans to the apparatus. In this way data is in control of the humans.

Out of 465 things that your marketing machine will do, eleven to fifteen are assigned to your humans, but humans still have to do their work.

As they say in the military, the Air Force can soften the targets, but the battles are won by the infantry. Your humans will have an obligation to consume this machine; I need their conceptual buy-in, and I need their heart in it. They will have to pick up the phone and call the prospect. They will have to close the deal. No matter how hard I work to perfect your paper, pixel, and plastic theater, your people will always remain your single biggest asset. And I don't program your humans, I only work on paper, pixel, and plastic.

Q. Why do you have a monthly maintenance fee?

A. Once your plan is built, where would you rather sit, in the cockpit or in the cabin where someone else is flying and you are minding your own business?

Most people want to outsource the day-to-day maintenance of a complex marketing machine that has a lot of moving parts. If you have the skills to manage an in-house or outsourced marketing management team, you will not need our monthly maintenance program.

Our process is not magical. It's all common-sense-driven. I have an assembly line approach. I can do something in one hour that will take you four hours. I have teams in India, America, and in multiple locations that work as one cohesive force that allows me to deploy your marketing management system day-in and day-out.

Imagine driving home from work, picking up the phone to call me, and saying, "Hey, I want to do campaign number 23 to list segment six in the next two weeks." You and I know exactly what we are talking about. That's what you get for monthly maintenance.

If you don't see a value in it or if you have someone else who can do the work that we do at the price we charge, we will cheerfully hand over the keys to your team. We will show them what we do; we will teach them how we do it, and we will be available as a backup if your team fumbles or needs something.

Or you might want to in-source everything internally, and have me as a consultant; then, you can talk to me about what you want to do differently today. You have a lot of options. We don't have a contract. The monthly maintenance is a month-to-month agreement. We bill on the fifth of every month. As long as you tell me on or before 30th of the month to stop charging you next month, then we will not charge you next month.

Q. Do you do SEO?

A. We don't do SEO; we don't do social media integration, and we don't do reputation management. These are highly-skilled traits that are meant for highly-trained professionals who are extremely good at them.

I am privileged to be teamed up with a sister company that eats, sleeps, and breathes SEO, social media, and reputation management. They come with the same passion for marketing and a money-back guarantee like me.

I will introduce you to their team, you will evaluate them; you will look at their rules of engagement, and you will make a decision whether or not you want to engage with them. If you hire someone else for SEO or social media marketing, we will collaborate with your vendor. We will team up with them; we will give them the call capture mechanism and the landing pages; we will facilitate the A/B Split testing, and we will team up with whoever does this part of the work.

Before you work with the team that we recommend to you, one thing you should know is that their team and our team are aware of each other's strengths and weaknesses.

Plus, you are also using the tribal buying power. Every time I get a client, our sister company gets a client. That way I have the capacity to pick up the phone and mediate if there is problem. Trust will never be an issue; if you can trust me, you can trust them. When we meet, I will make an introduction to you.

Q. Do you do printing?

A. Yes, we have a resident print production manager who will manage your printing, mailing, data processing, mail merge, and all that good stuff. We do not own our own print production facility. We work with a half-dozen vendors that have worked with in the past. We have trained them to work with us in an orthodontic environment. We buy their services wholesale, but for your production cost you are paying for your project manager, the production manager's time, a small contribution to my overhead, and a small profit. So you will spend about 20–30 percent more than the market.

Our rule of thumb is that if a project is larger than $5,000, it may make sense to ask one or more team members to do the coordination and management. In some cases, you will be using the same vendor as we will be using. If something goes wrong, we can take over the project and deal with any problems that are created by your team or mine. We just want it done, and as long as we are making our profits, we will manage.

Q. How do you integrate Infusionsoft with my practice management system? (For dentists)

A. If you go to DENTMA.com, it is a sister company of one of my fellow Infusionsoft ICP's, whom we talk with. If the bridge is small the system will extract data overnight. The campaigns are engineered to have APIs to trigger. What that means is that even emails can go automatically, as soon as I update the data from your practice management system.

If a bridge does not exist between your practice management system and Infusionsoft already, one can be built, for a small fee. You always rent the bridge; so it doesn't cost much to build a bridge; you just pay a small initiation fee and a monthly fee, and we will decide when and which bridge to buy. If you have multiple locations, you will need to buy multiple bridges.

Q. What do I do with the patient communication system I've got now?

A. We will look into it and what it is doing, and we will look at what Infusionsoft can do. Together we will decide whether or not you are going to keep that particular software in that particular role or not. Some of the functions can be shifted into Infusionsoft, so some of them will continue. Certain decisions will be made by you; some will be made by your staff; and some obviously we will decide if we are going to have that

or not. Sometimes we are going to have as few systems as possible, and that's the rule.

Q. How do you generate leads?

A. Targeted direct mail marketing
Internal marketing referral system
External referral marketing referral system
Online marketing
Social media
Targeted multi-step direct mail
Targeted every door direct mail
Internal client/patient referral marketing
External/co-marketing

Free-standing inserts
Pre- and post-event marketing

Q . What marketing methods do you NOT use?

A. As I said, we do not do online or social marketing; we do not do radio; we do not do television. We do not do public relations. We do not do space/print advertising. We do not do outdoor advertising, and we do not do vehicle wraps.

Q. What is your deal with Dan Kennedy?

A. Dan Kennedy jokingly calls me his parasite. If he is speaking somewhere and if I am allowed, I get inside the door and attend, and I will take detailed notes and prepare a mindmap.

If you have listened to him, Dan Kennedy is 30 percent core instructions on what you should do, about 40 percent anecdotal evidences, about 25 percent fun, and 5 percent picking on me, when I am in the audience. Without fail, that's how it works.

I mindmap the 30 percent of his core orders. From 2009 to 2019, I have over four dozen mindmaps with more than 8,000 direct instructions on what Dan Kennedy wants someone to do in their business. This is the raw material of my intelligence.

I implement what Dan Kennedy says from stage. If you are ever in the audience and Dan is speaking, you will listen; you will take notes; you will make circles; you will double underline some things, and then you will go home and transfer it to notebooks. I live in those notebooks. I draw technology, web, data, and production workflow to actually implement the spirit of Dan Kennedy.

I was a No B.S. Inner Circle by Advantage® Magnetic Marketing Advisor.

As a former MMA, I have access to lot of his learning materials, and I am always buying his stuff. I have the only Dan Kennedy library in the world. You can come to my office; we can sit on a couch, pick something from the bookshelf, and go through what Dan Kennedy said, and if you want a corresponding mindmap, I will print that out for you. That's my relationship with Dan Kennedy.

Q. Why do you always recommend Infusionsoft?

A. First of all, I don't ALWAYS recommend Infusionsoft. We are sort of "system agnostic." Our system can be implemented on almost any software, and we routinely use Hubspot, Infusionsoft, or Active Campaign. I have always been a systems implementation guy. I have worked on CRMs like Sugar CRM, Microsoft Dynamics, and SalesForce.com. I have done API on Sugar CRM. I have worked on Telematics. I have worked on Goldmine. I have worked on Oracle small business.

I have worked on multiple e-commerce platforms: Magento, Flipkart, etc. There are lots of shopping carts in the market. I have worked on several email marketing systems in the market, like Exact Target, Constant Contact, Vertical Response, etc. I love them all.

What I like about Infusionsoft is that it is a single SQL database that has tentacles in e-commerce, email marketing, response catcher, auto-response, marketing automation, and an open API, so that I can push/pull data into anything. There are other players in that field, and Infusionsoft happens to be the least expensive. It is $2,000 upfront + $300 per month depending on what applications you have. You can't beat that.

You hit the ground running, and I have all data in one place. It has integration with <u>Salesforce.com</u>, and with app exchange you can do almost anything. It has an API integration with your data in multiple SQL tables. How many places you want your data to be copied and stored? When you have one central database, it reduces your risk of data contamination.

Plus, I have a team that is wired to work on Infusionsoft. I have training materials, so I can train my people, my interns, and your staff members. Infusionsoft used to be a group of partners; they used to be called the Infusionsoft Certified Consultants (ICCs). I think now they are called Infusionsoft Certified Partners, and it's a small yet growing community of friends. I can put money on the table and reach out to any Infusionsoft consultant, who will move in and take care of any problem.

It's a great ecosystem; there are a few hundred of us, and there are tens of thousands of customers. There is enough business to go around, so ICCs are eager to help each other. They have built a culture of caring and sharing, and they have standardized the protocol for automation.

If you fire me and hire another ICP, somebody else will be able to pick that up and be able to run that. That's why I recommend Infusionsoft. I am familiar with it, I am comfortable with it, I like it, and it doesn't hamper my speed. Do I have a capacity to work on AWeber? Absolutely.

Do I have the capacity to work on Office Auto-Pilot? Sure, but I will probably talk you out of it.

Q. What is chaos to clarity?

A. Usually a business owner will want to have multiple conversations at the same time; therefore, they end up not describing anything. They might say, "I want to do social media, but before social media I need a website made, and how do social media and the website work together, and how am I going to capture the data?"—while the conversation was supposed to be about something else.

That is information chaos, and we all do it because a business owner's mind races million miles an hour. So, how do you go from chaos to clarity? The answer is by adequately mind mapping your thoughts. I use several software programs. I use software called <u>Mindjet.com</u> and <u>Geru.com</u>. These two applications (and other software) help me catalogue and display my thoughts, your thoughts, our thoughts, and anything that can and should be done for you. We also can mindmap the notes from a brainstorming session.

This allows the person to look at visual representation of their thoughts on the wall, so they can dive deeper into the specifics of what they want. It helps to rule out a bad idea as being bad, and it helps you jump from topic to topic and still catalogue what you had in mind. This is how you go from chaos to clarity.

Q. Who comes up with the content?

A. Content is a touchy subject. There are experts who know how to write, but someone needs to be skilled to capture the spirit of your practice and display it in a way that only you or someone better than you can display it.

You don't want to outsource it for the sake of saving time. You want to in-source it and seek the assistance of a content concierge who will help you follow Dan Kennedy's principles of persuasion. There are lots of books written on how to write content. Robert Cialdini wrote several books on the psychology of persuasion. Dan Kennedy wrote books and even has a formula for how to write content. You should study this material, so you are in the right mindset. You can write your own copy if you feel that you are comfortable, or our copy concierge will work with you.

Yes, we will have someone to write for you. It is not something we do internally; we have several writers who are trained to write with us. I am on a private client list for Dan Kennedy. I have an ability to hire writers from AWAI and Doberman Dan's Knights Club.

I have access to all kinds of copy writers, but there is the core team of writers that we work with very closely, and if you need assistance, we will give you a referral. Our prices do not include copy writers because we want the writer and client to work together directly. Content means copy, images that need to be purchased, and videos that need to be shot or bought. We will help you come up with what content you need, and then someone will come up with the content, but most of it will come from your heart.

Q: What if I need videos?

A: There are three kinds of videos:
You can take PowerPoint slides and add voice to it

You can have animated videos like what you see on my website Or someone can shoot you and edit the video Either way the procedure is same. There needs to be:
A purpose for the video
A storyboard for the video
Choreography for the video
Drafts you may need for the video
Scripts for the video
A rehearsal

We will help you think through these steps and then have someone who will do the work for you. You may have a videographer, or you may have a vendor in your area who is perfectly capable of shooting anything, but you need to give them the context, and we will be happy to provide that.

We also work with several studios in the country who understand our mindset. If we need to fly someone in to location, or fly you out to a studio, we can arrange that— but the cost to do anything on the video is usually not included in the price that we charge.

The consultation on the things that we do to help you come up with what you need for your video and all the other things we will be able to help you provide; that is included in the fee.

Q: How much work do I have to do?

A: A lot. Even though it is a done-for-you service, we are working on you. It is your business, so at times you will find the amount of work that you will have to do even after paying for our fees, you will find it frustrating. It is important that you understand your role and play your role well. If you don't, what we do for you will not deliver what it is supposed to do. So all in all, you should think about how much work you think you will have to do after you hire us—and triple that. We will help you manage your workload; we will nurture you in and out the project; we have systems in place to help you do what you need to do.

We have procedures, systems, and applications in place that will help you manage your workload. We will not leave you alone. We will tell you exactly what needs to be done, and someone will be there to assist you to do what you need to do, but you will have to do your share of work. There are certain things you just cannot outsource.

Q. Who is in charge of the process?

A. We are. We have a dedicated project manager, who will be running the project, and he will be in charge of the project management dashboard. You, your staff, and the other vendors will be reporting to this one master dashboard of the master task list. So, there will be one person who is in charge of everything at eLaunchers.

Q. Okay, what are some of the most common mistakes a dentist or orthodontist would make when either trying to do their own marketing or hiring another firm?

A. They don't begin with the end state or a goal state in mind.

They don't have a clear expectation as to what they want, what it will do for them, why it is important, and what is important about that.

The win conditions and the end state goals are not clearly defined.

The most important thing is they don't have an idea as to what constitutes the failure and what constitutes a successful implementation of a project.

One more thing most people don't do well is they don't plan. They don't plan out a project end-to-end or have an inventory of what needs to be done. This creates a situation where you don't have enough resources, you did not have enough capacity, you did not have enough money, you did not have enough time, or you just did not think through the project to get all the elements in place therefore your project will not deliver. This creates what we call a mess.

Q. There are lot of companies that claim to do a number of things that you do. Why are you better?

A. I don't claim to be better than anybody. I am who I am. I do what I do, and my clients love me for what I do. What I do is not rocket science; it is an applied common sense. I do what can and should be done for your business, and I help build an assembly line approach to marketing automation and marketing implementation.

A lot of companies understand marketing; some understand it better than me. Lots of companies do beautiful websites, some much better than me. Almost all of them can do better work than I can with the English language.

There are two things that I am better at than any other human in the world. I am a data scientist, and I understand the correlation between data and money better than anybody else.

While a lot of people can do something, and a lot of people know how to do something as good or better than me, you will find that I know what to do better than anybody else, but again I need to be humble about this.

Many people can do what we do, and they can do it extremely well, and some can do it for significantly less money than we can. So, you need to be 100 percent confident that this relationship that you and I are about to build together is really meant to be.

I don't want to engage in a relationship that you or I will regret, so if there is someone else who can do what I do that you are more comfortable with, then hire them for a portion of it, and if it does not work out, we will be happy to move in and clean it up for you. (We fix bad hair cuts.)

Here's how I look at what I do that is of value. We have three goals. We call them G0, G1, and G2. G0 is the goal of adding revenues and profits to eLaunchers. Any relationship we engage in should generate revenue for me and add to our profitability. That is my primary win condition, so I call it Goal 0.

The number one goal for you is to make our relationship a zero-sum game. In milestone one, I want to make you as much money as you paid me, so our relationship becomes a zero-sum game. That is the first thing I look for. Let's say you invested $35,000 with us. What are we going to do together so you sell $35,000 worth of your services? That is my goal number one.

My goal number two is three times the money you spent. If you spent $35,000, my G2 is $100,000 revenue for you.

With that $100,000, you are covering your overhead, and recovering your expenses of investment you made in me. You will also add money to your bottom line. With everything else that happens beyond that, you should be happy and grateful for the relationship that you and I have together.

So, it is not about why you would pick me over another competitor, it is about how you would measure if it was a good idea to hire me or not. Understand that I cannot guarantee success. I am in no way, shape, or form and phrase telling you that you will get G1. I am not telling you that you will get G2.

PRISM REFERRAL LETTER FROM DAN KENNEDY

From the desk of...

Dan S. Kennedy, Speaker, Author, Consultant

-

Something You Need To Know That Is SO IMPORTANT To Your Success In The Post-COVID Business Environment - I Decided To Introduce It To You Myself...

Hi, Dan Kennedy here,

If you've followed me for any length of time, you know I seldom write a letter like this. In fact, almost never. But this is so important, I did.

The enclosed letter from Parthiv Shah, *(written by master copywriter Russell Martino whose work I admire, and critiqued by me)*, is THE most important message I have seen go from one business owner to another in a long time.

I encourage you to read Parthiv's letter several times and circle the parts that apply to you and your business. And, I strongly encourage you to accept Parthiv's unique offer, which won't cost you a dime. And, will give you thousands of dollars' worth of TIMELY, ACTIONABLE INFORMATION, you can use immediately.

If your business has suffered because of COVID, it is not only in your best interest to read Parthiv's letter, it is URGENT that you stop what you are doing, and read the letter now. *I am certain you will be glad you did.*

If COVID has not damaged your business, it is still critical you read the letter carefully *so you have a clear understanding of how the best marketers, the ones who make selling high-dollar products and services look easy, make that happen.*

I agree with Parthiv's conclusion that failing to adapt to the changes the COVID pandemic has brought to life in the marketplace, WILL DESTROY FAR MORE BUSINESSES over the next year, than have been wiped away by this pandemic to date.

I agree COVID has, on a mass level, changed how people willing to spend money in the *POST-COVID Economy,* use the web to decide WHAT to buy. WHEN to buy.

And, WHO to buy from.

I agree that not adapting the changes detailed in the letter, may cost you a fortune in missed opportunity. And, I agree that adapting them, will give you a huge advantage.

With this said, I hope you enjoy the letter... I feel certain you will.

Dedicated To Multiplying Your Income,

Dan K

Dan Kennedy

GET GROWTH PRISM LETTER

The COVID ECONOMY changed how your prospects decide WHAT and WHEN to buy, and WHO they will buy from. Things will NEVER go back to the old way.

The only question is...

Will You Adapt & Prosper - Or Risk Everything & Die Online – Don't Be Left Behind – The Choice Is Yours...

Here's what you need to know...

In this letter...

- **FACTS:** How the Covid Pandemic forever changed how people use the web to determine WHAT they buy. WHEN they buy. WHO they will buy from. And, why, (without adaptation), this change may turn your web presence, and all your marketing assets, into a profit-killing liability that HELPS your competitors and HARMS your business.
- **RISK OF INACTION:** Why web pages that fail to meet the new consumer standards for making buying decisions, drive up the cost of marketing, waste leads, alienate good prospects, slow sales, kill optimism, and do more harm than good.
- **WHAT TO DO NOW:** Steps you can take TODAY to reach people IDEAL for your premium product or service. And, bring your web presence, sales letters and ALL your marketing assets up to the new standard, so people who find you through any means: SEO, paid traffic, and so on, take you seriously.

Dear friend and fellow business owner,

Right now, as you read these words, ***through no fault of your own***, your revenue, cash flow, peace of mind, and whether or not your business will survive for another year, are at risk.

How you respond to the facts revealed in the next few pages, will set your future in motion.

Your response to this letter may determine whether your next 12-months are a happy, high- profit event you are proud of. Or, a nightmare, business killing train wreck of a year you didn't believe could happen to you, and it's too late to undo.

Besides claiming over eight hundred thousand lives worldwide as of this writing, the COVID pandemic has sounded the death knell for over 100,000 business in the U.S. alone. Prosperous businesses that were doing well pre-COVID, now, are simply gone. Game over.

That's bad enough.

But what worries me the most is not what has happened.

What's past is past.

What worries me is, COVID changed everything.

And, failing to adapt to the changes will destroy FAR MORE GOOD BUSINESSES over the next year, than have been wiped away by this pandemic to date.

Like a tornado that sprang up out of nowhere, COVID landed you smack-dab in the middle of a NEW BUSINESS ENVIRONMENT WITH NEW RULES. Rules unknown to most business owners, unfamiliar to most marketing professionals, and unable to be implemented by all but a select few.

Fail to understand these rules, and everything will just get harder.

Fail to implement them effectively in your marketing, *and like so many others*, you risk suffering the humiliation of seeing everything you've worked for your entire business life, slip away.

This is maddening. Frustrating. Why should anyone, especially you, who have *paid your dues. Made sacrifices. Worked while others played. And, by sheer will and wits prospered while others failed... have to endure this!*

Worse yet, now, *at what should be the height of your earning power*, maybe for the first time in your career, you feel impotent. Powerless. Maybe even clueless about how to turn this around and get back on top of your game.

This is the last thing you need in your life! It's a tough pill to swallow. But, facts are facts. ***Everything's at risk!***

If you expect your *PIXEL ESTATE, which includes your* web site, funnels, landing pages, sales letters, blogs and *ALL YOUR MARKETING ASSETS*, both on and offline, to benefit you in ANY WAY through the end of Covid and beyond, this is the most important letter you will ever read.

And that's why, after you read every page, and see the facts for yourself, if you qualify...

...I will invite you to join me on a call where I will share how I helped a handful of Fortune 500 Companies in a similar situation after the World Trade Center bombings. **Hundreds of millions of dollars in sales were produced in matter of months,** while competitors dropped like flies, because they didn't know what to do in the post 9-11 environment.

More importantly, on this call I will share A NUMBER OF THINGS YOU CAN DO IMMEDIATELY, with or without my help, to stop the bleeding, attract excellent prospects for your premium product or service, and GET THEM TO CONTACT YOU, with questions answered. Objections handled. And, essentially READY TO BUY.

The more people who understand this, the better.

Here's what you need to know...

COVID has changed how people willing to spend money in the POST-COVID Economy, use the web to decide WHAT to buy, WHEN to buy, and WHO they will buy from.

These changes affect every business, including yours. *And, that goes DOUBLE for every business that sells a premium product or a high-dollar business or professional service.*

The Covid pandemic brought the U.S. economy to its knees.

> *"Over 100,000 small businesses are gone forever, and this is just the tip of the iceberg."* Source: a joint research study conducted by the University of Illinois, Harvard Business School, Harvard University and the University of Chicago.

Mark Zandi, chief economist at Moody's Analytics, predicts, *"Well over a million micro firms, (businesses with fewer than ten employees), will ultimately fail."*

Pew Research Center reports, *"Unemployment rose higher in three months of COVID-19 than it did in two years of the Great Depression."*

"Over 36 million people gainfully employed before the Coronavirus pandemic decimated the U.S. economy, are presently out of work." Source: New York Times

To help you appreciate the magnitude of what's happening, the 36 million people (the newly out of work in America), *is more than the **entire** population of Canada.*

Bottom line...

Small businesses are still dropping like flies, and it's going to get worse.

Millions are out of work, struggling just to keep food on the table.

The pool of people with enough money to buy any nonessential, big ticket product or service, is smaller now than at any time since the 2008 recession and shrinking by the minute.

And, that's just half the problem...

Far fewer people have disposable income for anything from elective dental, legal, chiropractic and medical services, to business services and premium products. ***And, people who can afford to buy what they want, are more reluctant than ever to spend money.***

And there's more...

Besides blowing a hole in the U.S. economy, skyrocketing unemployment, and shrinking the pool of possible buyers for virtually everything, the COVID pandemic has radically changed how everyone, (including your prospects), make buying decisions.

What worked in the past - does not work nearly as well today. **Companies that stick with pre- COVID style marketing, and fail to adapt, will NEVER recover.**

It's a brave new world.

What changed?

Before COVID decimated discretionary spending nationwide, most businesses competing in the same niche, had one thing in common: the entire focus of their web site, sales letters, emails, funnels, and so on, was the same: all about THE COMPANY and THE PRODUCT.

From a consumer point of view...

PRODUCT-CENTRIC and COMPANY-CENTRIC sales messages, ARE ALL THE SAME: graphically attractive, technically functional, with a STRIKINGLY SIMILAR message.

These kind of messages, on web sites, in sales letters, or wherever they are found - are all about the company and the product, hit none of the hot-button issues a good prospect would find engaging, and are riddled with meaningless self-serving statements everyone ignores - "we value our clients", "we put YOU first", "we are committed to excellence" – comments ANY business could make, from a company selling toilets, to a dentists selling a $40,000 full mouth restoration package.

> Most web sites offering similar products, or high-dollar business or professional services are so much alike in terms of LOOK, FEEL and CORE SALES MESSAGE (except for the name and logo), ***any company's online presenc***e is virtually interchangeable with any other company's online presence in the same niche.

Most sites in every niche – including yours - are so similar, if you check it out, you'll start humming the song "Little Boxes", with the lyric, **"They're all made out of Ticky-tacky and they all look just the same."**

The consequences of your **PIXEL ESTATE**, *(which included every word of copy a prospect might see, including; web site, funnels, landing pages, sales letters, blogs and ALL your marketing assets),* looking and sounding about like everyone else in your niche include;

1. PRICE becomes the only distinguishing factor, and;
2. If it all comes down to price: instead of being seen as a trusted authority WHO CAN SOLVE A PROBLEM YOUR BEST PROSPECTS DESPERATELY WANT TO SOLVE, they see you as just another look-alike company.

    So, why not go with the cheapest.

How is this possible? How can web assets in the same niche be so similar they are practically interchangeable?

Simple.

With few exceptions, tech wizards and graphic designers build your web site, *load prebuilt templates that all look about the same*, with minimal templated *'fill in the blanks'* copy that is all about the company or the product, (like a nice online brochure).

This process is so common, most business owners don't even question it.

But the fact that many people accept a **flawed process** as 'the norm' doesn't solve any of the problems this kind of flawed process, *or anything even remotely like it*, creates.

Here's what's real,

- Tech experts are great at coding. They make bells and whistles work.
- Graphic designers make PIXEL ESTATE ASSETS, *like web sites, funnels, landing pages and blogs, visually appealing.* Usually, by loading them up with stunning high-resolution photos – the kind you see in those slick, full-color brochures. *The kind nobody reads.*
- Most PIXEL ESTATES, including all the online assets, are designed, built, and have copy provided by **people who have never sold anything in their lives other than perhaps** their own professional services.

Tech wizards make things functional. Without them, nothing works. Graphic experts make things visually appealing. Without them, you look amateurish at best.

These experts play an important role.

BUT WHAT ABOUT WORDS THAT SELL? *What about content that* **GETS ATTENTION – HOLDS ATTENTION** *and* **COMPELS AN ACTION?**

- Which wizard creates compelling content that engages your prospects' interest, draws them into your site and gets them EXCITED about doing business with you? **The tech guy?**
- Who creates the content that makes your site ABOUT SOMETHING THE CUSTOMER CARES ABOUT, instead of all about the company or the product, or how long you've been in business? *Who does that for you?* **The graphic expert?**

- Who describes the problem in such detail, your prospects know for a fact you understand them? Who makes your story so compelling, your prospects come to see you as the ULTIMATE AUTHORITY, the one they want to do business with?
- Who crafts sales arguments so persuasive, they compel a response? Who weaves those arguments seamlessly throughout your web site, landing pages, and blog, so YOU become the clear choice for any real prospect, *and price becomes irrelevant?*

Who does all this for you?

Who crafts the messages that determine if your prospects RESPOND when they find you online – or CLICK AWAY in a few seconds, never to return?

In most cases, the answer is, NO ONE – at least no one with the kind of skill and expertise it takes to capture a prospect's attention. Engage their interest. And, convert a looker, into a buyer.

The content for most businesses' entire *PIXEL ESTATE*, is all about the company or the product. And, while that plays a role, **it has NOTHING to do with GETTING your prospects attention. HOLDING their interest. And, SELLING your product or service.**

That is why most sites in most niches are the same: visually appealing with lots of information about the company and the product. But, NOT engaging. NOT persuasive. And, NOT compelling enough to get a response, which begs the question, *'why choose you?'*

Over six short months, COVID changed the way people decide WHAT they buy - WHEN they buy & WHO they will buy from...

Before COVID struck, people had money and were willing to spend it.

The economy was booming. Unemployment was low. In general, people were optimistic and open to 'checking out' a product, service or company they were unfamiliar with.

Now, because of COVID, optimism is gone.

Businesses are struggling. Unemployment is sky-high. Fewer people have money.

And, those with money, are reluctant to spend it **on anything that does not solve a problem that is causing them pain today, or may cause them pain in the future**.

Simply put: your prospects are PROBLEM focused, not SOLUTION focused.

Talk to them about a problem they have *(or are at risk of having)*, and you get their attention. Start with anything else, like how long you've been in business, how great your company is, or even details on how your product or service works, *and you lose them FAST.*

This is not speculation. This is human nature. YOU CARE ABOUT WHAT'S IMPORTANT TO YOU. YOUR TIME IS VALUABLE.

You think about your business, your family, your health, your finances, goals you want to achieve, risks you want to avoid, things you want to have, things you want to do, and anything that may affect your life, or the life of a loved one.

Your prospects are the same.

How to get attention FAST.

If you want someone's attention, TALK ABOUT WHAT'S ON THEIR MIND. Anything else feels like an intrusion. An interruption. Something they just don't have time for.

If you have a problem, *(a hurt back, a bum knee, low energy, bad teeth, a rocky marriage, a job you hate, not enough money for retirement, slow sales, high cost of advertising, and so on)*, and that problem is causing you PAIN, and THAT PAIN is on your mind.

> Marketers who apply this, AND ENTER THE CONVERSATION GOING ON IN THE PROSPECT'S MIND, **sold circles around competitors who didn't know, or didn't know how to apply it,** *(in EVERY niche)*, **long before COVID struck.**

COVID is important, because, *(practically overnight)*, COVID changed the national mood from OPTIMISM to PESSIMISM, from CONSUMPTION to CONSERVATION.

"Not now!" is the national mantra for buying anything that's not a necessity.

And, since everyone considers getting out of pain, *(physical, emotional, or financial)*, and getting out of harm's way, a necessity...

> **...if you want to sell something, the key is to lead with the problem your product solves and the pain it relieves, BEFORE talking about the solution.**
>
> Do this well, and people with the PROBLEM and the PAIN, *will pay attention.*

COVID greatly accelerated the need for you to figure this out. Because in today's world...

If you fail to get your prospects' attention FAST - they WILL NOT ENGAGE in your content, and WILL BE GONE in seconds. *Another lead wasted.*

Response to email marketing, SEO and paid advertising slowed before COVID arrived. Those in the know, know people had stopped responding to anything that did not peak their interest.

Like it or not, if your marketing fails to get your prospect's attention and ENGAGE THEIR

INTEREST ON AN EMOTIONAL LEVEL, most of your marketing dollars, are wasted.

Now, with an uncertain future, and a reluctance to spend money, the most EFFECTIVE **way to get and hold a prospect's attention is...**

...See the world through your prospect's eyes. Understand the PROBLEM not having what you sell causes them. Understand the PAIN that problem creates. Then, craft content that makes it clear you understand their situation. You know, because you've been there. You solved the problem. And, you have a solution that may work as well for them, as it has for others.

This process is critical, because unless your prospect identifies with the problem your widget solves...the solution doesn't matter.

If you can't spell out the problem your prospect identifies with, and describe the pain it causes, they will NEVER buy your

solution, because they will never believe you truly understand their situation.

The consequences of NOT engaging your prospects on this level are devastating.

1. Your marketing is weak, not nearly as effective as it could be. Which means, you waste much of the hard-earned money you invest in marketing.
2. No one consumes your online content. For all the good it does, the information about your company and your product, may as well not be there.
3. Your SEO effort is wasted, because people who show up don't engage.
4. Your paid advertising drains your bank account and delivers a puny return, because without engagement, it doesn't matter how many people show up.
5. Your marketing helps your competitors more than you, because when a prospect fails to engage in your content, they just move on until they find something more compelling.
6. Your marketing costs skyrocket. Cost per lead soars. Cost per sale may double or triple. You spend more and work harder to earn less, with no fix in sight.
7. Sales decline. Cash flow is a problem. Profits vanish. You feel like the ship is sinking.
8. Stress and worry consumes you.
9. Your attitude sours. Your smile disappears. Your temper grows short. You feel alone and isolated. And, you begin to wonder if maybe your best days are past.

Every business owner experiences a few of these items at some point. It's shocking today, how many entrepreneurs and professionals with good businesses, and a long track record of success, have made it all the way to number nine on this list and not recovered since COVID struck.

How much of this applies to you?

Are you concerned with the current situation?

Is your business growing the way you planned? Are you reaching your goals?

Is the financial future you imagined when you started your business on track? Or, have things gone sideways, and now, if you don't pick up the pace, you'll never reach your goal?

Do you have a good product or service that solves a real problem, but no matter what you do or how much you spend to reach good prospects, it seems like no one is paying attention?

Has the marketing that worked well enough for you pre-Corona, slowed to a crawl? Do you wish finding good prospects was easier? Do you wish selling was easier?

Do you wish your marketing was strong enough that people would consume your content, and then contact you with questions answered, objections handled, and essentially ready to do business?

Are you frustrated because costs are high, sales are slow, nothing you try to solve the problem works all that well - and you wish you could find a solution?

If you have any of these concerns, there's good news.

It doesn't have to be that way.

There is an ACTIONABLE SOLUTION ***to increase prospect engagement practically overnight***. And, transform your

PIXEL ESTATE, *(web site, funnels, landing pages, blogs, and so on)*, into an INCOME PRODUCING ASSET, you can rely on.

In just a minute, I'll share details on how to make that transformation and begin enjoying the benefits. But first, allow me to introduce myself.

Hi, my name is Parthiv Shah.

I am the President of eLaunchers.com, one of the top digital marketing agencies in the country.

We help business owners and professionals who sell premium products and big-ticket business or professional services, *get maximum benefit for every dollar they invest to build their business.*

Niches we serve: all big-ticket business and professional services, including, dentistry, legal, financial, chiropractic, alternative medicine, cyber security; high-dollar coaching and training programs, securing investors for exempt Reg-D offers, and more.

Since 1989, I've worked with thousands of business owners, handled over 10,000 direct response marketing projects. And, mailed over one BILLION pieces of direct mail on their behalf. During that time, I developed and implemented direct marketing campaigns, (on and off line), that have generated hundreds of millions of dollars in revenue for clients ranging from small professional practices to Fortune 500 Companies.

My first goal with a client is to determine who buys from you. Why they buy. And, what they must believe before they buy FROM YOU.

With this information, I build systems to reach your ideal prospects. Engage attention, and *get them to TAKE THE*

NEXT STEP. resulting in more sales, more cash flow, a great ROI on your marketing, and an impressive bottom line.

These are not idle words.

As a DATA SCIENTIST, I have a superpower that gives you a tremendous advantage.

I never guess WHO your ideal prospects are. And, I never guess WHERE to find them. The result: **every communication eLaunchers sends, (on or off line), goes to a virtual clone of your BEST customers or clients the... ones who PAY, STAY and REFER.**

The Power of Data Unleashed

Imagine the kind of explosive growth you'd enjoy, if every marketing message your send, online and off, reaches people IDEAL for your premium product or service.

Get a strong message in front of ideal prospects, and more people engage. More respond. And, more buy. **Nothing will grow a business faster.**

As a Data Scientist with a reputation for making clients' money, a Fortune 500 Company engaged me to develop a process to identify the best possible prospects for their products and services. *And, I did.*

Here's the story...

The World Trade Center bombing is a dark spot in our history, a horrific event that shocked everyone, and brought business and commerce to a screeching halt.

Much like the COVID pandemic, this paralyzed the nation. Planes were grounded. People were scared. Discretionary spending evaporated. It hit the economy like an atomic bomb.

Overnight, hundreds of thousands of businesses, large and small, were tossed head first into a nightmare scenario many would not survive: a business disruption resulting in higher costs, fewer sales, and consumers reluctant to spend money on anything but necessities.

No business can survive those conditions for very long. And, it wasn't long before companies

run by people who understood the seriousness of the problem, began to act.

A Fortune 500 Company
Reaches Out For Help

In response to the business disruption following the World Trade Center disaster, a Fortune 500 Company hit the panic button. Being familiar with my reputation as a Data Scientist capable of solving marketing problems most couldn't even guess how to solve, they engaged me to find a way to *"cut marketing costs"* and simultaneously, *"increase sales"*.

In other words, SPEND LESS to EARN MORE.

Besides improving efficiency and cutting unnecessary costs, the BEST way to SPEND LESS and EARN MORE, is; 1) FIND BETTER PROSPECTS, and; 2) deliver a stronger, more engaging message that *GETS ATTENTION* and *COMPELS A RESPONSE.*

To find those IDEAL prospects, I developed the proprietary **PRISM Research Method™**. *And, the results were spectacular!*

A number of my Fortune 500 and Global 500 clients, including BMW, Volvo, CVS, Gillette, and Reebok, launched new, post 911 marketing campaigns BASED ENTIRELY ON MY PRISM LIST RESEARCH, *that generated hundreds of millions of dollars in sales, in about a year.*

Results this good don't stay under wraps for long. Word got out. And soon, companies of all sizes and descriptions were waiting in line for me to implement PRISM Research for them.

PRISM research gives you an unprecedented advantage in the marketplace. It gives you the ability to reach out across a community, city, state or nation, and, *with laser-like accuracy, identify people IDEAL to benefit from your premium product or service.*

With that advantage, you have no limits. You can reach IDEAL prospects at will. You can grow as fast as you like. You can double your business. And, double it again, if you want.

How You Can Benefit From the Same Process Fortune 500 Companies Use To Identify People IDEAL For Their Premium Products and Services

eLauncher's clients benefit from the same PRISM Research Method™ these companies, who still use the *PRISM Research Method™* today, paid a fortune for me to create.

Using PRISM, I identify *the 20% of the customers responsible for 80% of your sales revenue over the last year.* These are your very best customers or clients, the ones you wish everyone was like. And yes, one way or another, the eighty-twenty rule always applies.

Next, I create a data driven avatar of exactly who those IDEAL prospects are. Data fields that may be considered, include age, sex, income, home owner, value of home, type of automobile, credit score, American Express card holder, real estate investor, stock market investor, zip code, magazine and newspaper subscriptions, and many more.

Then, using prestigious data sources, including SRDS, D&B, Reference USA, Acxiom, Equifax, Experian and others, I locate your ideal prospects, *ONLINE* and *OFFLINE*. And, implement custom marketing campaigns, *(complete with automated follow up and long term nurture)*, that generate a ROBUST STREAM of excellent prospects who, **depending on the impact of your content,** are pulled into your copy where they become convinced YOU are RIGHT for THEM.

PRISM solves one of the biggest problems you'll ever face in business; **finding an unlimited number of prospects IDEAL for your premium product or service.**

But, it takes more than a good prospect to make a sale.

Finding Great Prospects Is Step One... WITHOUT CONVERSION – YOU HAVE NOTHING

Once you find a great prospect, the sale, (and your business), will LIVE or DIE **based on the strength of your marketing message** in whatever form it is found. *(Sales letters, web site copy, emails, funnels, landing pages, videos, blog, special reports, white papers, and so on).*

If your message fails to engage your prospects, if your copy fails to draw your prospects into

your world... so they can discover WHY you are different, HOW you can help, and why your solution is superior, they'll be gone in seconds. *And, all your effort is wasted.*

As an agency owner, I struggled with this problem.

PRISM, makes finding great prospects easy. But, that's only half the battle. Once you find them, you have to get their attention. Hold their interest. And, convert the looker, who reads your messages, into a buyer who becomes a raving fan and gives you referrals. That's the goal.

But all too often, the letter, web site, email or blog article the client provides is weak. Lackluster. Not engaging. All about the company or the product – *with no hot-button issues that would draw a good prospect into the copy and compel a response.*

This was not acceptable!

A chain is as strong as the weakest link.

And, my goal is to make is to make my clients a fortune.

Putting good prospects in front of weak copy that fails to engage, is a losing proposition. It costs you money. It poisons the well. It gets the prospect to *'write you off'* in their mind.

Even worse, it primes that prospect to keep looking, until they find something more engaging, no doubt, on a competitors' site. *There's nothing like funding the competition!*

I had to solve this problem.

I needed a strategy to measure the persuasive impact of a client's sales letters, emails, web copy, blog, and so on – BEFORE we invest in new lead generation. That way, if the copy is not engaging, if it misses the mark, we can replace it with STRONG copy that engages the prospect.

In short, I needed a reliable process to identify **hot-button issues** that grab a prospect's attention and pulls them into the content, like a tractor beam on the Starship Enterprise.

> ...With this information, the writer has what they need to WRITE COMPELLING COPY that holds a prospects interest – so they consume your message, and take the next step, whatever that may be – **set an appointment, watch a video, download a report, request more information... or BUY your widget.**

After a few false starts, *(and spending a fortune trying to solve this problem)*, I discovered the TOOL and developed the PROCESS that accomplishes all this, and more.

THE PRISM
Why People Buy
Discovery Process...

With this unique process, I determine the GAINS your prospects want to achieve, the PAINS they want to avoid, and the Jobs To Be Done for them.

Next, I examine your **VALUE PROPOSITION.** I analyze your products and services *through the lens of HOW THEY CREATE GAIN and/or RELIEVE PAIN, and how they* **'do the jobs that need to be done'** *for the prospect to get what they want.*

When your VALUE PROPOSITION matches your prospects' GAINS TO ACHIEVE, PAINS TO AVOID, and JOBS TO BE DONE, there is a fit. ***And, we will have uncovered the hot-button issues that GET and HOLD a good prospect's attention.***

This was the missing piece.

With hot-button issues that are ALL ABOUT THE PROSPECT, spelled out, the copywriter has the firepower it takes to write strong, engaging copy that gets and holds attention.

Copy that rises to this level, draws good prospects into your world.

The wizards of marketing, persuasion, and sales agree: if you want to persuade someone to do something, ***like take a serious look at your product or service***, you must;

1. **Understand what your prospects want**, *which is never a product or a service.*

2. ***Understand the PROBLEM they face and the PAIN it causes,*** *including why they have the problem, why most solutions fail, and why yours is different.*

3. ***Then, craft content that pushes those buttons, pulls your prospects into your world, and demonstrates you understand their problem, and have a solution that may work well for them, as it has for others.***

This is how you ENTER THE CONVERSATION IN YOUR PROSPECT'S MIND. *And, when you enter that conversation with this level of understanding, you EARN your prospects attention. They see you as an authority. And, are happy you arrived in their life!*

Tools for Explosive Growth
PRISM Research = PROSPECTS

PRISM Why People Buy Discovery Process = COPY THAT SELLS

1. **The PRISM Research Method™**, identifies your ideal prospects, people who are virtual clones of your best customers or clients, the ones who PAY, STAY and REFER, the ones you wish everyone was like.

2. **The PRISM – Why People Buy - Discovery Process**; 1) nails down the problems, the pain and the emotions your prospects experience. 2) Identifies the gains they want and the jobs to be done for them to avoid the pain and enjoy the gain. And; 3) details how your product solves the problem, eliminates the pain, and gives the customer the gains they want.

Arm a copywriter with this information, *and they have what they need to write compelling copy that pulls prospects into your world. And, gets a response.*

> Together, these unique processes, give you the power to transform your PIXEL ESTATE, *which includes every word of copy a prospect may read online of offline,* into an **ACTIVE INCOME PRODUCING ASSET** that drives growth, and gives you maximum return on every dollar you invest to build your business.

These tools take the guess work out of growing your business. Together, they skyrocket the probability of your marketing campaigns being a huge success and delivering an excellent ROI.

Great Leads + Strong Content = Growth

Put great leads in front of customer-centric content, and good things happen.

1. Replace weak company-centric, product-centric copy, with strong CUSTOMER- CENTRIC MESSAGING, *and the probability of your marketing message getting and holding a good prospect's attention, especially in troubled times, soars.*

2. A strong message loaded with hot-button issues on problems and pain your prospect is dealing with, demands attention.

3. With stronger copy and better engagement, your return on SEO, paid advertising, offline to online promotions, and so on, will improve.

4. Putting great prospects in front of compelling content will bring you more sales, lower marketing costs, higher profit, and jealous competitors.

5. With strong sales and cash flowing into your business like a river after a huge rain, your attitude will improve. You'll smile more. And, instead of feeling like your day has come and gone, you'll feel like you're just getting started. *And, the BEST is yet to come!*

Why am I sharing this with you?

Simple. I hold a belief that dates back to the French Revolution, and popularized in modern times by the late great Stan Lee through his character Peter Parker.

"With great power - comes great responsibility."

The COVID pandemic has ended lives. Killed dreams. And, put millions out of work. COVID has changed the way people buy. The old way is gone, never to return.

As upsetting as this may be, and as angry as it may make you: without adapting to WHAT WORKS NOW, and making changes to your marketing copy, wherever it is found, online or offline, you risk becoming a statistic, instead of a wealthy business owner who does what it takes to SURVIVE and PROSPER beyond all expectation.

Fortunately, for you, your employees, your family and your future customers or clients, it's not

too late. There is a fix. And, it's not as difficult as you may imagine. You still have a choice.

You can adapt, upgrade your sales message, and prosper, perhaps more than ever.

Alternatively, you are free to struggle with rising costs, and suffer with weak sales until things get so bad, you just give it up -- and, become further proof of what Charles Darwin said in Origin of Species in 1859: **species that fail to adapt to a changing environment, die.**

With the knowledge I possess, my experience solving these kinds of problems, and the insight I can share, *you can adapt, and, march confidently into your most profitable years ever.*

Without that knowledge, *the same knowledge I use to generate hundreds millions of dollars in sales for clients,* the risk is: **your neck may be on the chopping block.**

Bottom line: I CAN HELP and am HAPPY to do so - that's why, for *business owners* who qualify, I opened a LIMITED number slots in my schedule each week to discuss this.

Questions you are sure to have...

Will stronger copy give you a sustainable sales boost?

Who writes the copy once the **Why People Buy Discovery Process** is complete?

Will the upgraded copy work in customer reactivation campaigns? What about email sequences and funnels? What about sales letters, blog articles and special reports?

Do I have to start over with copy? Or, can I solve the problem by adding **A FEW KEY PAGES** that connect with the prospect and make the site more engaging?

Will changing FROM company-centric TO customer-centric copy that details the PROBLEM and the PAIN prospects experience, bring my PIXEL ESTATE in line with what people respond to today?

How does focusing on the problem and the pain increase engagement? Don't people want to know about the company and the product before they buy? Do emotional hot-buttons matter all that much? Can the PRISM Research Method locate leads in any geographical area?

How does this process transform my PIXEL ESTATE, (web presence, email sequences, funnels, blog, and so on), into a **DEPENDABLE INCOME PRODUCING ASSET?**

Can I do this without you? Or, do I have to hire you to get the results I want?

If I decide I want eLaunchers to implement my Growth Master Plan, how much does it cost? When can we start? What's included? How long does it take? Is there a guarantee?

How do I get these answers?

WHAT'S THE NEXT STEP?

Your Next Step couldn't be easier.

Pick up the phone and call, or go online and schedule an initial Growth Master Plan Discovery Call. This call takes about 20 minutes.

This is so important, I arranged things so I can take a **limited number** of these calls each week and spend the time necessary to answer your questions, and develop a plan you can follow, *with or without my help,* to PROSPER in these challenging times.

During the call, we spend a few minutes getting to know one another. Then, I answer your questions. And, ask a few of my own to determine your most pressing needs.

If there's a fit between <u>YOUR PRIMARY GROWTH NEEDS,</u> and HOW I CAN HELP, the next step is to schedule two, one-hour **Growth Plan Sessions**, to develop a **GROWTH MASTER PLAN** for your business.

This sounds like a tall order. And, maybe it is. Even so, we'll get it done. We'll stay on track. And, *I GUARANTEE, you'll find the process enjoyable, and extremely valuable.*

There is no cost, charge or obligation of any sort for these two calls.

What Happens On Call One...

<u>Your first one-hour growth planning session is about STRATEGY.</u>

1. We examine your business economics, including; where you stand in terms of total revenue, profit per transaction and a great deal more. And, we evaluate your process for attracting new business, your sales process once a new lead arrives, the lifetime value of a new customer or client, and a great deal more.

2. Next, we examine your **Value Proposition.** I analyze your products and services *through the lens of HOW THEY CREATE GAIN and/or RELIEVE PAIN,* and see how well that lines up with the gains your prospects want to achieve, and the pains they want to avoid. In the process, we uncover hot-button issues that will get and hold attention, and determine if they are present and how effective they are in your current PIXEL ESTATE.

3. Next, we determine WHERE YOU ARE, *your current state in terms of sales and profit in your business.* Then, you decide WHERE YOU WANT TO BE, (goal state).

4. Next, we work out how much incremental growth you need quarter by quarter to reach your growth goal on schedule. We evaluate your conversion rate, (turning lookers into buyers). And, we determine how many new leads you need quarterly, monthly, and weekly to reach your revenue goal.

5. Then, given your desired outcome, *(determined in step four above),* you tell me your plan, as you currently see it, to reach your goal.

This is a lot to accomplish in an hour, but with the process we follow, an hour is all it takes to get the answers needed for a HIGHLY PRODUCTIVE second call.

The second call, which typically happens the next day, is all about PLANNING.

During your second one-hour Growth Planning Session, we...

1. Evaluate different strategies to accelerate your growth. We evaluate the EASE of each possible solution, the IMPACT of each solution, and the

PROBABILITY OF SUCCESS of each solution under consideration. Then, we choose the growth strategy or strategies best suited for your situation.

2. Next, we develop a Quarterly Tactical Operational Plan, QTOP. The outcome of this process is a step-by-step activity plan to reach your goals, using the chosen strategy. This operational plan becomes your ROAD MAP FOR ACCELERATED GROWTH.

3. Next, we review the project planning tools we use at eLaunchers.com to oversee a project, keep track of weekly activities, and make certain the things that are supposed to happen, do happen ON TIME, ON BUDGET and ON SCOPE.

4. Next, you see case studies and examples of what we've done for clients in similar situations. And, discuss the results they experienced over what time frames.

5. Finally, we discuss where to go from here: your next steps to reach your growth goals, if you see eLaunchers.com as a good fit to help you grow, and what happens if you do.

Your outcomes for putting your business under this kind of FACT FINDING, GOAL SETTING, PROBLEM SOLVING microscope, include;

- You will have a clear picture of your business economics; cost per lead, cost per sale, your current revenue vs. your desired revenue, the lifetime value of a new customer or client, how many leads and sales you need to make up the difference, and more.
- You will understand your VALUE PROPOSITION in terms of the problems your customers experience and the pain they want to avoid. And, you will have a list of HOT BUTTON ISSUES that will get and hold

a good prospects attention, and in many cases, get the desired response.

- You will have EXTREME CLARITY on where you are in your business today, and where you want to be in the time frame of your choosing.
- You'll have a Quarterly Tactical Operational Plan, *(QTOP)*, and spreadsheet detailing the most powerful steps you can take to move from your CURRENT STATE to your GOAL STATE with the HIGHEST PREDICTABLE DEGREE OF SUCCESS.
- You'll know the best project management tools available, all of which are accessible to you whether we work together or not.
- You will know from the case studies we review, exactly how well the growth strategy you believe is best for you, worked for others in a similar situation. And;
- By the end of the second call, you will know if you would like eLaunchers.com to drive the process for you and implement the plan we developed.

If it turns out we work together, great, we'll discuss details and get started.

If not, we will have had a great time working on your business. You'll have valuable insights you can apply right away. And, who knows, maybe we'll work together at some time in the future.

Either way, this will be time well spent!

Is this your best course of action? Is making the call and investing two hours to work on your business right for you?

Darwin replies...

A short summary of Darwin's theory: SURVIVAL OF THE FITTEST. Species best suited to their environment tend to survive and prosper, while others less suited, struggle and fail.

Said another way: Species that fail to adapt to a changing environment, go extinct. They die out. Pass away. And, cease to exist, while species that successfully adapt, prevail and prosper.

The environment you do business in, has changed.

Your prospects' priorities have changed.

How your prospects decide who they will do business with, has changed.

The kind of messages your prospects respond to, have changed.

> And your competitors, the ones that have not died out and are determined to prevail, are working overtime to figure out the changes, and adapt, *so they can have their best years ever going forward, and grab customers or clients who may have easily been yours... if only you had adapted first.*

Survival of the fittest is alive and well.

You accepting my offer, and allowing me to lead you through the *Free Growth Planning Process,* (*typically reserved for clients who pay thousands of dollars to get started*), *may be the most significant, most valuable thing you can do to ADAPT and PROSPER going forward.*

The two hours of time you invest going through this process, will give you an advantage most businesses, including your competitors, simply don't have.

- You'll have a Road Map to follow, a strategic plan to optimize everything, and sell more of your premium product or service starting right away.
- You'll have a perfect understanding of WHAT'S WORKING NOW.
- You'll know how to achieve fail-safe implementation.

And it won't cost you a dime!

That about wraps it up, except to say...

<u>With prospects ideal for your premium product or service, strong copy, a well thought-out growth plan, and the ability to implement, there's no limit to what you can accomplish. This is the Holy Grail of direct response marketing.</u>

And, this is what your Growth Planning Session is all about.

- Developing a plan to implement these elements in your business,
- Finding an endless supply of ideal prospects for your premium product or service,
- Developing a compelling message prospects will respond to.
- Detailed insight on how to achieve fail-safe implementation... and more.

This is what ever business needs, but few have. This is the secret sauce that can put you on track for enjoying your most profitable years going forward.

I hope you find this valuable, and accept my offer.

To schedule your 20-minute Discovery call: phone **301-760-3953** or to schedule online, visit **elaunchers.com/start** and pick a time convenient to your schedule.

It will be a pleasure get to know you.

Sincerely and all the best,

Parthiv Shah
President, eLaunchers.com
www.eLaunchers.com
email: pshah@elaunchers.com

Cell: 301.873.5791 (Feel free to text me, I will respond promptly)

PS – that number again is **301-760-3953** – or schedule online at: www.GetGrowthMasterPlan.com

PPS – Just a reminder, there is no cost, charge, or obligation of any sort for hopping on the phone with me and working on your Growth Master Plan. I honestly believe *'with great power comes great responsibility'.* And I know from long experience, *and a portfolio of excellent results,* accepting my offer and going through the process will pay HUGE dividends.

PPPS – If this is right for you, and you want to schedule a call, now is the time.

I am delighted to answer your questions, evaluate your data, uncover hot-button issues that will get people to respond to your content, and develop a Growth Master Plan, *(you can implement with or without my help),* to bring you more business fast.

But with all the responsibilities of running eLaunchers, and making sure clients reach their quarterly revenue goals and stay on track to enjoy their best year ever... I can only carve out enough time for nine (9) new Growth Planning

Calls a month... *and this letter is going to land on the desk of over 1492 business owners in the eLaunchers.com database over the next few weeks.*

So again, if this is for you, go ahead and schedule now so we can get started, and you don't have to wait in line for no telling how many weeks.

Call **301-760-3953**, or schedule online at: **www.GetGrowthMasterPlan.com**

13236 Executive Park Terrace
Germantown, MD 20874
301.760.3953
pshah@eLaunchers.com
www.businesskamasutra.com

Made in USA - North Chelmsford, MA
1262787_9780990505921
05.20.2022 1523